Disney

COOKING WITH MAGIC
A CENTURY OF RECIPES

Disney
COOKING WITH MAGIC
A CENTURY OF RECIPES

INSPIRED BY TEN DECADES OF DISNEY'S ANIMATED
FILMS FROM *STEAMBOAT WILLIE* TO *WISH*

INSIGHT
EDITIONS

SAN RAFAEL • LOS ANGELES • LONDON

CONTENTS

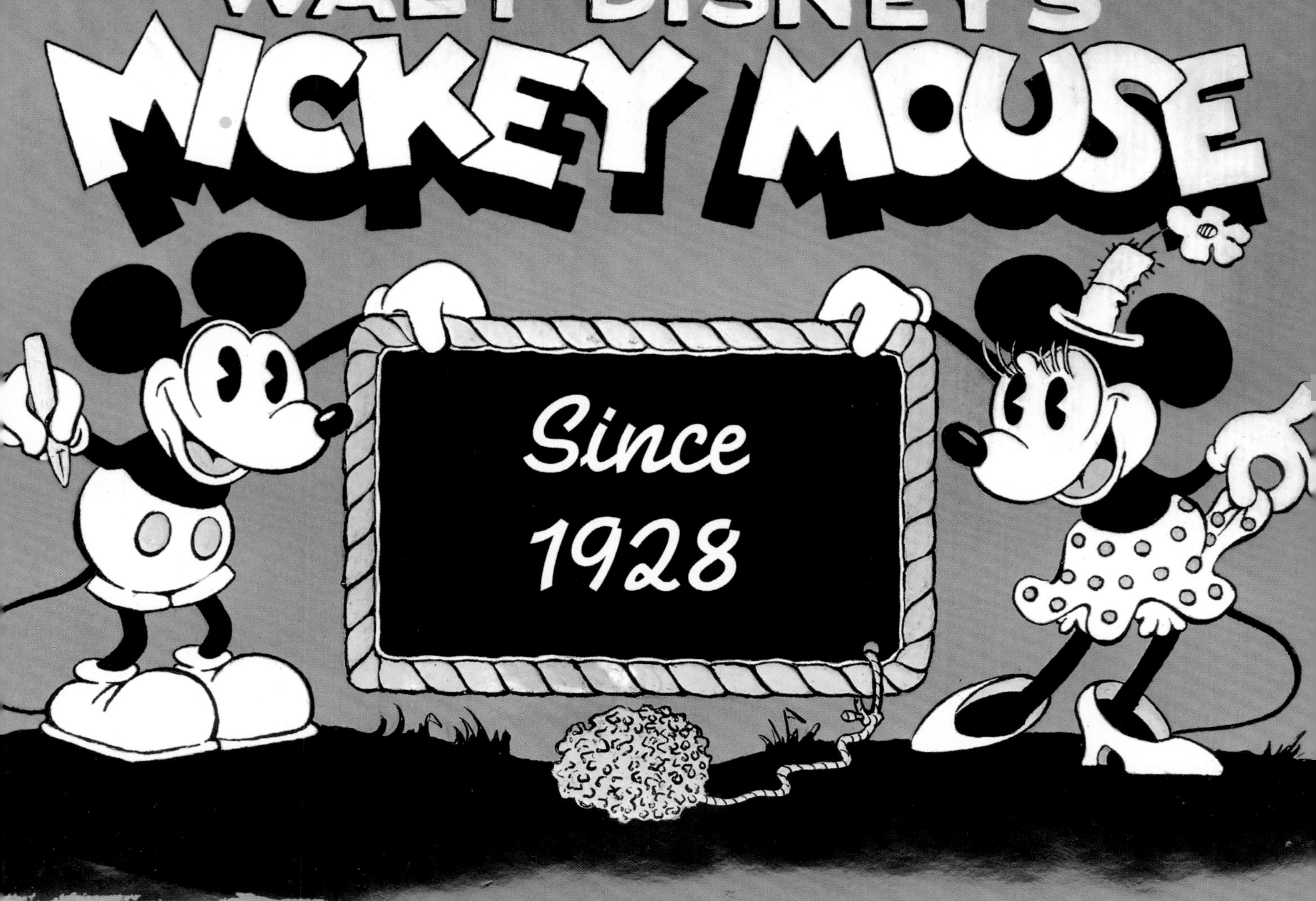
WALT DISNEY'S
MICKEY MOUSE
Since
1928

INTRODUCTION

Originally founded as the Disney Brothers Cartoon Studio in 1923 by brothers Walt and Roy O. Disney, the Walt Disney Company has entertained and inspired people around the globe for over a century. Through the power of its unparalleled storytelling, Disney is the most globally recognizable animation studio in the world.

The concept of family and friendship, in all varieties and permutations, is a unifying theme across nearly every Disney animated film, in a line stretching from the title characters in 1933's *Three Little Pigs*, to the group of friends who stand up for each other in 2023's *Wish*.

Disney films often highlight the shared meals that act as a force to unite families and friends. Winnie the Pooh surrounds himself with his closest pals, who rally together to face all sorts of challenges—and share honey. Snow White cooks dinner for her newfound friends, the miners. Belle and the Beast's journey to love begins over a shared breakfast after he saves her life. Timon and Pumbaa share their problem-free philosophy with Simba, teaching him (and fans) that "home is where your rump rests," while bonding with the lion cub over slimy, yet satisfying, grubs. And the Madrigals and the Guzmáns come together to join their two families over a sumptuous meal, secure in the knowledge that Julieta can heal anyone with her culinary creations.

As we watch these animated films time and again—perhaps while enjoying delightful bites with our own families and friends— we're reminded of connection, and how we can nourish the important people in our lives not just with food, but with support, encouragement, and love.

With this book, we'll explore the history of Disney, decade by decade and recipe by recipe, with a detailed look at how Disney grew from a small company to the entertainment giant it is today. Inspired by Disney's beloved characters, this collection of more than 75 recipes celebrates a century of magnificent Disney animation.

So, be our guest! While you and yours watch—and rewatch—your favorite Disney animated films, you can be inspired to cook your way through a century's worth of Disney recipe magic.

TIMELINE OF FILMS

1928:
STEAMBOAT
WILLIE

1933:
THREE LITTLE
PIGS

1934:
THE WISE
LITTLE HEN

1934:
THE GODDESS
OF SPRING

1935:
THE GOLDEN
TOUCH

1951:
ALICE IN
WONDERLAND

1949:
THE ADVENTURES
OF ICHABOD AND
MR. TOAD

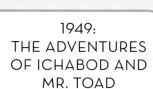

1947:
FUN AND
FANCY FREE

1950:
CINDERELLA

1942:
BAMBI

1940:
PINOCCHIO

1937:
SNOW WHITE
AND THE SEVEN
DWARFS

1941:
DUMBO

1940:
FANTASIA

**1953:
PETER PAN**

**1991:
BEAUTY AND
THE BEAST**

**1955:
LADY AND
THE TRAMP**

**1959:
SLEEPING
BEAUTY**

**1989:
THE LITTLE
MERMAID**

**1988:
OLIVER &
COMPANY**

**1961:
ONE HUNDRED
AND ONE
DALMATIANS**

**1981:
THE FOX AND
THE HOUND**

**1963:
THE SWORD
IN THE STONE**

**1977:
THE RESCUERS**

**1967:
THE JUNGLE
BOOK**

**1970:
THE ARISTOCATS**

**1973:
ROBIN HOOD**

**1977:
THE MANY
ADVENTURES
OF WINNIE
THE POOH**

1992:
ALADDIN

1994:
THE LION
KING

2005:
CHICKEN
LITTLE

2007:
MEET THE
ROBINSONS

2004:
HOME ON
THE RANGE

1995:
POCAHONTAS

1996:
THE HUNCHBACK
OF NOTRE DAME

2003:
BROTHER
BEAR

1997:
HERCULES

2002:
LILO &
STITCH

1998:
MULAN

2002:
TREASURE
PLANET

2000:
THE EMPEROR'S
NEW GROOVE

2001:
ATLANTIS:
THE LOST
EMPIRE

2008:
BOLT

2009:
THE PRINCESS
AND THE FROG

2010:
TANGLED

2012:
WRECK-IT
RALPH

2013:
FROZEN

2023:
WISH

2021:
ENCANTO

2016:
MOANA

2014:
BIG HERO 6

2022:
STRANGE
WORLD

2021:
RAYA AND
THE LAST
DRAGON

2016:
ZOOTOPIA

HELPFUL TOOLS

BLENDER: Blends or purees sauces and soups to varying textures, from chunky to perfectly smooth. Also used to make smoothies and shakes.

BOX GRATER: A four-sided tool featuring different grating surfaces on each side. Used to shred cheeses or firm fruits and vegetables, and to finely grate the skin of citrus fruits.

CANDY THERMOMETER: Sometimes called fry thermometers, these long glass thermometers can be clipped to the side of a pot. They can withstand temperatures of at least 500°F and are used to measure the temperatures of frying oil or sugar when making syrups, candies, and certain frostings.

COLANDER: Separates liquids from solids by draining the liquid through the small holes in the bowl.

DUTCH OVEN: A large (usually 5- to 6-quart) heavy cooking pot ideal for making stews, braises, and deep-fried foods. Dutch ovens are often made from cast iron or enameled cast iron, which makes them hold and distribute heat evenly. A Dutch oven works well when cooking with both high and low temperatures, making it a versatile vessel and handy addition to every kitchen.

DRY MEASURING CUPS: Measuring tools that usually come in sets of ¼ cup, ⅓ cup, ½ cup, and 1 cup sizes. They are ideal for measuring dry ingredients such as flour, sugar, rice, and pasta.

FOOD PROCESSOR: A motorized machine with a bowl and a series of removable blades used for chopping, shredding, slicing, and blending ingredients. A food processor can be used to prepare vegetables, fruits, and cheeses for cooking as well as blending sauces and dips.

FRYING PAN: Shallow round cooking vessel used primarily for stovetop cooking. It's good to have a range of sizes. Generally, a small skillet is 6 inches across; a medium skillet is 8 inches across; a large skillet is 10 inches across; and an extra-large skillet is 12 inches across.

HAND MIXER: A lightweight handheld machine with removable attachments used for blending and whipping eggs, cake batters, and lighter-weight, less-dense doughs.

HIGH-HEAT VS. NONSTICK PANS: A high-heat pan—as its name suggests—can stand up to high-heat cooking, generally temperatures between 400°F and 600°F. They're usually made of stainless steel, cast iron, or enameled cast iron and can be used on the stovetop or oven—if the handle is made of an ovenproof material. Nonstick cookware contains a coating that helps keeps foods from sticking (particularly eggs), but they can't be used at the same temperatures as high-heat pans. If you are cooking with nonstick cookware, make sure you know the manufacturer's heat limits for your cookware. Most nonstick cookware should not be used at above medium heat on a stovetop (about 350°F) and is not generally suitable for the oven.

IMMERSION BLENDER: A handheld machine used for pureeing soups and sauces in the pot.

LADLE: A cup with a long handle used for serving soups and stews and transferring liquids.

LIQUID MEASURING CUP:
Clear glass or plastic measuring tools used for measuring precise amounts of liquids by lining up the level of liquid to the marks on the cup. Useful sizes include 1 cup, 2 cup, and 4 cup.

MEASURING SPOONS: A set of measuring tools used to accurately portion smaller amounts of ingredients. They usually come in a set that includes ⅛ teaspoon, ¼ teaspoon, ½ teaspoon, 1 teaspoon, and 1 tablespoon. They can be used for liquid ingredients such as vinegar, juices, oils, and extracts, and dry ingredients such as flour, salt, sugar, and spices.

MUDDLE: A short-handled tool that is textured on one end used to mash together ingredients such as fruits, herbs, and sugar when making flavored drinks.

PARCHMENT PAPER: Food-safe paper that can withstand temperatures of up to 450°F—even up to 500°F for short baking times—that's used to line pans for baking and roasting. Parchment paper keeps foods from sticking and makes cleanup easier.

ROLLING PIN: A long, cylindrical tool—most often made of wood—used to flatten and roll out dough when making breads and pastries.

RUBBER SPATULA: A handled tool with a flat, flexible blade used to fold ingredients together and to scrape the sides of bowls clean.

SAUCEPAN WITH LID: Round deep cooking vessel used for boiling or simmering. It is useful to have a range of sizes, including a 1 quart, 2 quart, 3 quart, and 4 quart.

SILICONE BAKING MAT: Used to line shallow baking pans when making foods such as cookies and pastries to prevent sticking. They can withstand high temperatures in the oven and can also be used in the freezer. Dough can be rolled out on them, and they can easily go from prep station to chilling to the oven without having to move the dough. They are easy to clean and reusable.

SPATULA/PANCAKE TURNER: A handled tool with a wide, flexible blade used to flip or turn foods during cooking.

STAND MIXER: A heavy-duty machine with a large bowl and various attachments used to mix, beat, or whip foods at varying speeds. Stand mixers are necessary for making heavy, dense, or stiff doughs for cookies or yeasted breads.

WHISK: A handled tool with thin wires arranged in various shapes used for mixing and whipping liquids and batters. The two most common types of whisks are the balloon whisk, which has a bulbous end that narrows down toward the handle, and the sauce whisk, which has a round coil that sits flat on the bottom of the pan.

INGREDIENTS AND TECHNIQUES

BUTTER: Unless otherwise noted, recipes call for salted butter.

BUTTERFLY PEA FLOWERS: These dried flower blossoms are commonly used in herbal tea drinks. When added to a recipe, they provide a beautiful deep blue color. If combined with acids, like lemon juice, the color turns to pink or purple. They are available online and in some health food stores. They are also turned into a powder and an extract.

DEMERARA SUGAR: A partially refined brown sugar, its color and flavor falls somewhere between granulated sugar and light brown sugar.

EGG WASH: A mixture used to create a sheen or gloss on breads, pastries, and other baked goods. Whisk together 1 egg and 1 tablespoon of water until light and foamy. Use a pastry brush to apply before baking when the recipe requires.

GRANULATED SUGAR: A highly refined sugar made from sugar cane or beets known for its white color and fine texture. All of the molasses has been removed from this type of sugar.

LUSTER DUST: An edible, food-safe glitter used to decorate cookies, cakes, and other types of pastry. It can be mixed with a clear alcohol to create a shimmery paint or brushed on dry. It can be purchased online or in specialty baking departments.

MILK: Unless otherwise noted, these recipes call for dairy milk. In most cases, any percentage of milk fat will do, unless otherwise indicated.

PEELING GINGER: To peel fresh gingerroot, use the edge of a small spoon to scrape away the peel. This keeps the root intact, with less waste, and allows you to easily navigate the lumps and bumps.

POWDERED SUGAR: Also called confectioners' sugar, this is granulated sugar that has been ground into a powdered state. It's primarily used to make smooth icings and for dusting finished baked goods.

PURPLE POTATOES: There are more than 1,000 varieties of potatoes grown around the world, and purple (or blue) potatoes are among them. They have a dense flesh and nutty flavor and can be boiled, mashed, roasted, grilled, or fried. If you can't find them, substitute with Yukon Gold potatoes.

SALT: Unless otherwise noted, use your salt of choice in the recipes in this book. Kosher salt—which is coarser than regular table salt—is the type of salt that is most commonly used throughout the book.

SUMAC: Commonly used in Mediterranean and Middle Eastern cooking, this spice made from the ground berries of the sumac flower has a fruity and slightly tart, lemony flavor. It is great for use in dry rubs, marinades, and dressings. It adds not only flavor but a beautiful warm reddish-pink hue to foods.

VANILLA PASTE VS. VANILLA EXTRACT: Vanilla bean paste provides strong vanilla flavor and beautiful vanilla bean flecks without having to split and scrape a vanilla bean. While it is more expensive than extract, there are situations in which it really elevates the finished dish. When that's the case, a recipe will specifically call for vanilla bean paste, but it can always be replaced in a 1-to-1 ratio with vanilla extract.

CHAPTER 1

1923–1949

Full of imagination and a passion for entertainment, Walt Disney and his brother Roy founded the Disney Brothers Cartoon Studio in 1923, which was later renamed the Walt Disney Studio in 1926. Walt and Roy spent their early years successfully creating short animated films for other studios. But Walt had dreams for himself that were more than just producing shorts for other companies.

In 1927, while working with Charles Mintz, who had a distribution deal with Universal Pictures, Disney and one of his top animators, Ub Iwerks, created a character for Mintz that would be owned by Universal. Tired of seeing the ever-popular animated cats, they decided to make their new creation something different: a rabbit. Oswald the Lucky Rabbit was an instant success, which was very exciting for Disney and Iwerks, reinforcing that the Disney studio had the talent and ability to succeed in animation. But there was a problem: Walt didn't own the rights to Oswald—Universal Pictures did. So, in 1928, Walt Disney parted ways with Mintz, unfortunately leaving the lucky rabbit behind.

Undeterred, Walt knew that he could create an equally endearing character of his own. And he did. The character was named Mickey Mouse. On November 18, 1928, Walt released the animated short *Steamboat Willie*. It was the first animated short to feature synchronized sound throughout, an incredible technological accomplishment for the time. From the opening scene showing Mickey whistling as he steers the boat along the water to the final scene showing Mickey laughing, every action had a sound effect precisely tied to it. This new character and the use of the new technology were an instant hit!

Following the success of *Steamboat Willie*, Disney released another groundbreaking film in 1937: *Snow White and the Seven Dwarfs*. Not only was *Snow White* the first full-length animated film to be released in Technicolor, but it is still celebrated today for its compelling story that allowed it to hold its own against traditional live-action films. But the good times were not immediately to continue for Walt Disney and his studio, now named Walt Disney Productions: World War II was coming, and its impact limited the global distribution of the studio's ensuing theatrical efforts, such as *Pinocchio* (1940), *Fantasia* (1940), *Dumbo* (1941), and *Bambi* (1942). The Disney studio was forced to take a step back. With many of its animators off fighting in the war, Walt Disney Productions pivoted its focus to creating films that supported the war effort, including military training films and package features such as *Saludos Amigos* (1943) and *The Three Caballeros* (1945). However, Walt Disney was not discouraged by these challenges and kept his chin up, knowing that he'd one day be able to return to creating beloved animated feature films.

LOUISIANA FRIES

If Mickey Mouse learned one thing during his stint as *Steamboat Willie*, it was how to peel potatoes! After all, all that dancing and playing music is hungry work, and someone has to prepare dinner! The parrot Mickey chased off may have been laughing at him by the time his adventure was over, but no one would *dare* laugh at this recipe. They might ask for seconds, though!

SIDE DISH ✦ GF, V ✦ YIELD: 4 servings

Salt

2 pounds russet potatoes, cut into 1-inch cubes (peel on)

4 tablespoons butter

4 cloves garlic, minced

3 tablespoons vegetable oil

2 tablespoons chopped fresh curly leaf parsley

Black pepper

Preheat oven to 400°F. Bring a large pot of generously salted water to a boil. Add the potatoes and bring up to a simmer. Cook the potatoes for 5 minutes. Drain well and spread out on a large rimmed baking sheet to dry.

While the potatoes are drying, place the butter in a small saucepan. Add the garlic and place the pan over very low heat. Allow the butter to melt slowly. Cook the garlic, stirring frequently, until just softened—do not allow to take on color—about 8 to 10 minutes. When the garlic has softened, remove the pan from heat.

Heat a large ovenproof skillet over high heat (cast iron is ideal). Add the oil and heat until shimmering. Add the potatoes. Shake the pan gently to coat the potatoes with the oil. Cook, without stirring, until the potatoes start to crisp, about 2 minutes. Stir gently, then cook for 2 minutes more.

Transfer the skillet to the oven. Cook until the potatoes are crispy and golden, 10 to 15 minutes.

Remove the skillet from oven. Add the parsley to the hot garlic butter. Spoon the butter over the potatoes. Season with black pepper and additional salt to taste. Serve immediately.

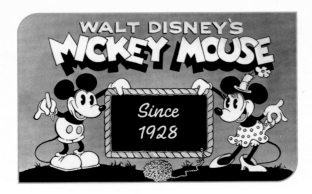

1928

STRAW AND HAY PASTA

The Three Little Pigs all have their own ideas about what would make a great house. But it's the house made of straw and hay that manages to get finished first. Taking its inspiration from the first little pig, this tasty dish is fast and easy to make—just like his house. And it's sure to leave you huffing and puffing for more!

ENTRÉE ✦ V ✦ YIELD: 4 servings

8 ounces dried plain fettuccine

8 ounces dried spinach fettuccine

½ cup butter, cut up

1 cup heavy whipping cream

2 cups freshly grated Parmesan cheese, divided

Salt and ground black pepper

3 ounces plant-based bacon, cooked according to package directions and chopped

1 cup frozen peas, thawed

Chopped fresh parsley

Cook the plain and spinach fettuccine together according to package directions.

While pasta is cooking, in a large skillet, combine the butter and cream. Heat over medium heat until just hot but not boiling, and the butter is melted. Stir in half of the cheese and add salt and pepper to taste.

When pasta is done, drain, reserving about 1 cup of the cooking liquid. Immediately add the hot pasta to the skillet. Toss with tongs to coat the pasta. If sauce is thick, add pasta-cooking water, 1 tablespoon at a time, until you achieve the desired consistency.

Stir in the chopped "bacon" and peas. Stir in the remaining cheese. Transfer to a serving bowl.

Garnish with parsley and additional black pepper.

1933

BUTTERMILK-HONEY SKILLET CORNBREAD

Famously known as the first appearance of Donald Duck, *The Wise Little Hen* is a short not to be forgotten! When the Wise Little Hen asks Peter Pig and Donald Duck for help with planting her corn, the two claim to have stomachaches. Later, when she asks for help watering, harvesting, and baking her corn, they again tell her they don't feel well. So, it's no wonder that the Wise Little Hen doesn't share her cornbread with them. But, luckily, our recipe is made for sharing! Whether you're eating alone or sharing, this rich cornbread is hen-tastic!

BREAD ✦ V ✦ YIELD: 8 to 10 servings

2¼ cups fine yellow cornmeal

2 cups buttermilk

¼ cup olive oil

¼ cup butter, cut up

2 large eggs

2 tablespoons honey or sugar

1 teaspoon baking powder

1 teaspoon baking soda

1 teaspoon finely chopped rosemary (optional)

¾ teaspoon salt

Butter and honey, for serving

Heat the oven to 450°F.

Spread the cornmeal evenly on a shallow rimmed baking sheet and toast in the oven until it begins to brown lightly on the edges, about 5 minutes. Transfer the hot toasted cornmeal into a large bowl; add the buttermilk and stir until combined; set aside.

Heat a 10-inch cast-iron skillet (see note) in the hot oven for 5 to 10 minutes.

Remove the hot skillet from oven. Add the olive oil and return to the oven to heat the oil, about 5 minutes. Remove before the oil begins to smoke. Add the butter to the hot skillet, whisking together the oil and butter until melted. Tilt the skillet to oil the sides of skillet. Pour all but about 1 tablespoon of the oil mixture into the cornmeal mixture. Add the eggs, honey, baking powder, baking soda, rosemary, if using, and salt to the cornmeal mixture. Stir well to combine.

Pour the cornmeal mixture into the oiled, hot skillet. Bake until the top is cracked and edges are lightly browned, about 15 minutes. Cool for 10 minutes before serving.

Cut into wedges and serve with additional butter and honey.

> **NOTE:**
> If you don't have a cast-iron skillet, any oven-safe skillet will work.

1934

SPRING SALAD WITH GREEN GODDESS DRESSING

As the Goddess of Spring, it's Persephone's job to oversee all of the plants that bloom and perhaps even vegetables that ripen in the spring. But poor Persephone only gets to spend six months of the year above ground before returning to the underworld. Luckily, Persephone would surely make the most of her time by turning her harvest into a delectable salad, complete with edible flowers, similar to this one!

SIDE DISH ✦ GF, V, V+* ✦ YIELD: 6 servings

FOR THE DRESSING

½ cup fresh parsley leaves

1½ cups baby spinach leaves

3 tablespoons chopped chives

1 tablespoon chopped fresh dill

2 cloves garlic, minced

1 tablespoon Dijon mustard

Zest and juice of 1 lemon

1 tablespoon white wine vinegar

½ cup canola oil

½ cup mayonnaise

FOR THE SALAD

One 5-ounce package mixed spring baby lettuces

1 cup sugar snap peas, thinly sliced

½ cup fresh English peas or frozen peas

4 to 6 spring radishes (French Breakfast, Easter Egg, Watermelon, Purple Plum), thinly sliced

3 rainbow carrots

1 cup fresh pea shoots or microgreens

Fresh ground black pepper (optional)

Edible flowers, such as pansies, violas, violets, or borage

MAKE THE DRESSING:

In a blender, combine the parsley, spinach, chives, dill, garlic, mustard, lemon zest and juice, vinegar, oil, and mayonnaise. Blend well, stopping to scrape the inside of the blender with a rubber spatula as needed. Place the dressing in a glass jar with a lid and chill until needed.

MAKE THE SALAD:

In a large bowl, toss together the lettuces, sugar snap peas, English peas, and radishes. Peel the carrots and cut into ribbons with a vegetable peeler. Divide the lettuce mixture among 6 salad plates. Top each pile of greens with carrot ribbons and pea shoots. If desired, grind a little black pepper over each serving.

Garnish with edible flowers. Serve with the dressing.

> **NOTE:**
> To make this dish vegan, use vegan mayonnaise.

1934

GOLDEN TOUCH ROASTED CHICKEN

King Midas has a special gift. Everything he touches turns to gold—even his food! Make your own Midas-like dinner with this oven-roasted chicken that looks golden on the outside but is perfectly juicy on the inside. The golden touch of this recipe will treat you like royalty!

ENTRÉE ✦ GF ✦ YIELD: 6 servings

6 small bone-in, skin-on chicken breasts

¼ cup buttermilk

2 tablespoons lemon juice

2 tablespoons honey

2 cloves garlic, minced

1 teaspoon ground turmeric

½ teaspoon salt

¼ teaspoon cayenne pepper

1 cup uncooked Emperor's (or forbidden black) rice

2 cups chicken broth

1 teaspoon olive oil

2 green onions, thinly sliced

Place the chicken pieces in a 1-gallon resealable plastic bag. In a small bowl, combine the buttermilk, lemon juice, honey, garlic, turmeric, salt, and cayenne. Spoon over the chicken in the bag. Remove air from the bag and seal. Move the chicken around in the bag to coat evenly. Refrigerate at least 2, but up to 24, hours.

Heat the oven to 475°F.

Line a large shallow baking pan with foil. Place the refrigerated chicken, skin-side up, on the prepared baking pan. Do not remove excess marinade from the chicken. Bake the chicken until golden brown and no longer pink in the center (160°F), 25 to 30 minutes.

Meanwhile, rinse the rice in a fine-mesh sieve until the water runs clear. In a medium saucepan, combine the rice, chicken broth, and olive oil. Bring to a simmer over medium-high heat. Reduce the heat to low. Cover and simmer 30 minutes. Remove from the heat (do not remove the lid) and let stand for 10 minutes to steam. Stir in the green onions.

Serve the chicken over the rice.

1935

SAFE-TO-EAT APPLE STRUDEL

Although the evil Queen poisoned Snow White with a magically poisoned apple, there are many very delicious—and *safe*—ways to prepare apple-flavored treats. This Safe-to-Eat Apple Strudel, inspired by the apple Snow White fatefully bites into, won't leave you awaiting true love's kiss, but rather awaiting a second helping!

DESSERT ✦ V ✦ YIELD: 8 servings

FOR THE DOUGH

1 tablespoon granulated sugar

⅛ teaspoon salt

¼ teaspoon baking powder

1 large egg plus 1 egg yolk, beaten

4 tablespoons butter, very soft

¾ to 1 cup all-purpose flour, plus more for dusting

Heat the oven to 400°F.

MAKE THE DOUGH:

In a medium bowl, combine the sugar, salt, baking powder, egg and egg yolk, and the butter. Gradually stir in enough flour to make a soft dough that forms a ball. On a lightly floured surface, gently knead the dough for about 5 minutes until smooth and elastic. Cover and set aside.

continued on page 31

1937

continued from 28

FOR THE FILLING

¼ cup whole milk, plus more for brushing pastry

⅓ cup sour cream

½ teaspoon vanilla extract

⅓ cup plus 1 teaspoon granulated sugar, plus more for sprinkling on pastry

1 pound baking apples, such as Cosmic Crisp, Golden Delicious, or Granny Smith

¼ cup golden or regular raisins

½ teaspoon ground cinnamon

2 tablespoons all-purpose flour

1 tablespoon butter, melted

FOR SERVING

Powdered sugar

MAKE THE FILLING:

In a small bowl, whisk together the milk, sour cream, vanilla, and 1 teaspoon sugar.

Peel and thinly slice the apples. Place the apple slices in a large bowl and toss with the raisins, remaining ⅓ cup sugar, cinnamon, and flour.

Cut a piece of parchment paper to fit the bottom and up the sides of a 15-by-11-by-1-inch jelly roll pan. On a work surface, lightly dust the parchment with some flour. Turn dough out onto parchment paper. With a well-floured rolling pin, roll out the dough to make a thin rectangle, about 1 inch from edges of parchment paper, adding more flour as needed so the dough doesn't stick to the parchment. Spread the sour cream mixture evenly over the center of the dough, leaving a 2-inch border around edges. Spoon the apples evenly over the sour cream. Drizzle the apples with the melted butter.

Fold one of the long sides of dough toward the center, stretching it slightly, to cover most of the apples. Fold the short edges of dough toward the center, covering some of the apples. Brush the last long edge of dough lightly with water and fold it toward the center, stretching it slightly and overlapping the dough to cover all of the remaining apples. Gently roll the log over so that seams are underneath. Use a sharp knife to cut a few slits across top of log. Brush the top of the log with a little milk and sprinkle lightly with sugar.

Transfer the parchment and log to the jelly roll pan. Bake for 10 minutes. Reduce heat to 350°F and bake until the apples are tender and pastry is golden, about 30 minutes more.

Let cool on the pan for at least 30 minutes before serving. Carefully transfer to a serving platter using spatulas. Serve warm, dusted with powdered sugar.

BLACK FOREST HOT COCOA

The forest can be a dark, scary place—especially when you're all alone. Inspired by Snow White's night in the forest, this cup of hot chocolate is sure to warm your bones after a night spent in the woods!

DRINK ✦ GF, V ✦ YIELD: *4 servings*

3 ounces good-quality bittersweet chocolate, chopped

⅓ cup plus 2 tablespoons granulated sugar

2 cups whole milk, divided

¼ teaspoon almond extract

½ cup 100% cherry juice

¾ cup heavy whipping cream

Chocolate shavings

4 candied dark cherries (premium cocktail cherries)

In a medium saucepan, combine the chocolate, ⅓ cup sugar, and ½ cup of the milk. Cook, stirring constantly, over medium heat just until mixture comes to a boil. Stir in the remaining 1½ cups milk. Remove from heat. Stir in the almond extract and cherry juice.

In a medium bowl, beat the whipping cream with the remaining 2 tablespoons sugar until stiff peaks form. Spoon into a piping bag with a large star tip.

Ladle the chocolate mixture into 4 mugs. Pipe whipped cream on top of each mug. Sprinkle with chocolate shavings and top each with a cherry. Serve immediately.

1937

TUSCAN ROAST CHICKEN

After a long day of making puppets for the children in his little Italian village, Geppetto is ready to share a hearty dinner with Pinocchio, Cleo, and Figaro. Luckily, he knows just how to make one. From a roasted chicken to a table full of side dishes, Geppetto cooks like he's got a whole family coming to dinner. Perfect for eating alone or sharing with a family, you won't be lying when you say this tasty chicken is delicious!

ENTRÉE ✦ GF ✦ YIELD: 4 to 6 servings

FOR THE CHICKEN

One 3- to 4-pound whole roasting chicken

1 lemon

2 sprigs fresh sage, divided

2 sprigs fresh thyme, divided

3 cloves garlic, smashed and peeled

3 tablespoons olive oil, divided

Salt and ground black pepper

FOR THE POTATOES

1 pound tiny mixed new potatoes, halved

2 cloves garlic, thinly sliced

2 tablespoons olive oil

Salt and ground black pepper

1 tablespoon Dijon mustard

2 tablespoons freshly grated Parmesan cheese

FOR SERVING

Fresh sage, thyme, and lemon wedges, for garnish

Heat the oven to 375°F.

MAKE THE CHICKEN:

Pat the outside and cavity of the chicken dry with paper towels. Halve the lemon and place both halves inside the chicken cavity along with 1 sprig of sage, 1 sprig of thyme, and the garlic. Tie the legs together with kitchen string. Twist the wing tips under the back. Place the chicken, breast side up, on a rack in a shallow roasting pan. Brush with 2 tablespoons of the olive oil and sprinkle generously with salt and pepper.

Roast, uncovered, until the chicken is no longer pink (165°F for breast meat and 175°F for thigh meat), 75 to 90 minutes.

Meanwhile, chop the remaining sage and remove thyme leaves from remaining sprig. In a small dish, combine the herbs and remaining 1 tablespoon olive oil. When the chicken is done, brush the herb mixture over the entire chicken. Let the chicken rest for 10 minutes before serving.

MAKE THE POTATOES:

Combine the potatoes and garlic in a 13-by-9-by-2-inch baking pan or small rimmed baking pan. Drizzle with the olive oil. Toss to coat. Sprinkle generously with salt and pepper. Place in the oven alongside the chicken. Roast potatoes until tender and browned, 30 to 40 minutes, turning the potatoes once with a metal spatula halfway through roasting.

When done, toss the potatoes with the mustard and sprinkle with Parmesan cheese.

Serve the chicken and potatoes on a platter. Garnish with additional herbs and lemon wedges.

1940

WALTZ OF THE FLOWERS FAIRY CAKES

There's nothing more moving than watching a group of fairies flutter across your screen to the score of *Waltz of the Flowers* from Tchaikovsky's *The Nutcracker Suite*. But watching it with your own "fairy cakes" as snacks only enhances the experience. So called in England, these cupcakes make the perfect complement to any *Fantasia* viewing.

DESSERT ✦ V ✦ YIELD: 12 fairy cakes

FOR THE FAIRY CAKES

1 cup all-purpose flour

1 teaspoon baking powder

2 large eggs, at room temperature

1 cup granulated sugar

½ cup whole milk

2 tablespoons butter

FOR THE FROSTING

½ cup heavy whipping cream

1 tablespoon granulated sugar

1 tablespoon sour cream

½ teaspoon vanilla extract

Powdered sugar, for dusting

Edible small flowers, such as violas, borage flowers, or fairy roses

MAKE THE FAIRY CAKES:

Heat oven to 350°F. Line 12 standard muffin cups with paper liners; set aside.

In a small bowl, stir together the flour and baking powder. In a large bowl, beat the eggs with an electric mixer until slightly thickened and lemon colored, about 4 minutes. Gradually add the 1 cup granulated sugar, 2 tablespoons at a time, beating on medium-high until pale yellow and thickened, 4 to 5 minutes. Beat in the flour mixture on low just until combined.

In a small saucepan, heat the milk and butter over low just until the butter is melted. Add to the egg mixture, folding in lightly to combine. Pour the batter evenly into the prepared muffin cups. Bake until the cakes bounce back when lightly touched in the center, 12 to 15 minutes. Remove the cupcakes from the pan and cool completely on a wire rack.

MAKE THE FROSTING:

For whipped frosting, in a medium bowl beat the whipping cream, sugar, sour cream, and vanilla with an electric mixer until stiff peaks form. Place the frosting in a piping bag fitted with a large star tip.

To decorate fairy cakes, use a small sharp knife to remove a round concave disc from the top center of each fairy cake. Angle the knife to get a disc that is ¼ inch in the center. Cut each disc in half to make fairy wings. Pipe a swirl of whipped frosting in the divot of each fairy cake where the tops were removed.

Stick a pair of wings into each swirl of frosting. Dust fairy cakes lightly with powdered sugar and decorate with an edible flower. Store in the refrigerator, uncovered, up to 4 hours.

1940

THE SORCERER'S APPRENTICE WIZARD-HAT CUPCAKES

When Mickey Mouse finds the Sorcerer's hat left unattended, he can't help himself. Slipping it on, he tries his hand at replicating the Sorcerer's magic. Unfortunately, magic isn't that easy, and Mickey soon finds himself in over his head—literally. Luckily, making these delicious cupcakes is far easier than wrangling hundreds of out-of-control brooms! A sugar cone and some blue frosting, and you'll be well on your way to your own kind of magic!

DESSERT ✦ V ✦ YIELD: 12 cupcakes

FOR THE CUPCAKES

1 cup all-purpose flour

½ teaspoon baking soda

¼ teaspoon salt

½ cup boiling water

⅓ cup dark or black unsweetened cocoa powder

⅓ cup chopped bittersweet chocolate or semisweet chocolate chips

¾ cup granulated sugar

½ cup sour cream

½ cup vegetable oil

2 large eggs

1 teaspoon vanilla extract

MAKE THE CUPCAKES:

Heat oven to 325°F. Line 12 standard muffin cups with cupcake liners; set aside.

In a small bowl, combine the flour, baking soda, and salt. In a large bowl, combine the boiling water, cocoa powder, and ⅓ cup chopped chocolate. Whisk until smooth and chocolate is melted. Whisk in the sugar, sour cream, oil, eggs, and vanilla until combined. Stir in the flour mixture just until combined.

Divide the batter evenly among the prepared muffin cups, filling each cup about two-thirds full. Bake until a toothpick inserted in the center comes out clean, 18 to 20 minutes. Remove cupcakes from muffin pan and cool completely.

continued on page 40

1940

continued from 39

FOR THE WIZARD HATS

One 16-ounce can white frosting, divided

Concentrated blue gel food coloring

12 cone-shaped ice cream cones

Gold Stars and Moons (recipe follows)

FOR THE CHOCOLATE GLAZE

½ cup chopped bittersweet chocolate or semisweet chocolate chips

3 tablespoons unsalted butter

FOR THE GOLD STARS & MOONS

White fondant

Powdered sugar

½ teaspoon gold luster dust

2 teaspoons vodka

MAKE THE WIZARD HATS:

Tint frosting a deep royal blue. Place about ½ cup of the blue frosting in a small piping bag. Set aside.

Place remaining blue frosting in a small microwave-safe bowl. Microwave on high just until melted and pourable, 20 to 30 seconds.

Holding an ice cream cone from the inside over the frosting bowl, spoon blue frosting over the cone to cover, allowing excess to drip off. Place point-side up on parchment paper to dry. Repeat with remaining cones. If frosting becomes too thick, return to microwave and heat for 10 seconds until melted.

MAKE THE CHOCOLATE GLAZE:

Microwave the ½ cup chopped chocolate and butter on high for about 30 seconds. Stir and microwave until melted and smooth, another 15 to 30 seconds.

When wizard hats are dry/set, spread about 1 tablespoon chocolate glaze on top of a cupcake. Place a wizard hat on top of wet glaze to stick. Repeat with remaining cupcakes, glaze, and hats.

Snip the tip from end of piping bag with white frosting. Pipe a band of icing around base of cones.

MAKE GOLD STARS AND MOONS:

Roll out a small amount of white fondant on a surface lightly dusted with powdered sugar. Use small or very small cutters to cut out stars and moons. In a tiny bowl, stir together ½ teaspoon gold luster dust and 2 teaspoons vodka. Brush gold paint on stars and moons. Let dry about 1 hour or until no longer sticky. Attach to the blue cones with a small dab of blue frosting.

FRIENDSHIP-BUILDING PEANUT BARS

When Timothy Q. Mouse sees Dumbo lying all alone, he decides that he will be the little guy's friend. But how can he get an elephant to trust a mouse? By offering Dumbo a peanut as a token of friendship, it isn't long before the two are the best of friends. And you'll be making friends, too, with anyone you offer these delicious peanut bars to!

DESSERT ✦ V ✦ YIELD: 18 bars

FOR THE BARS

Vegetable oil, for greasing pan

1 cup all-purpose flour

1 cup granulated sugar

¼ teaspoon salt

½ cup butter

¼ cup creamy peanut butter

½ cup hot water

¼ cup buttermilk

1 large egg, lightly beaten

½ teaspoon baking soda

½ teaspoon vanilla extract

½ cup finely chopped roasted peanuts

FOR THE FROSTING

⅔ cup creamy peanut butter

4 tablespoons butter, melted

½ cup powdered sugar

1 teaspoon vanilla extract

½ cup finely chopped roasted peanuts

MAKE THE BARS:

Heat the oven to 350°F. Grease a 13-by-9-by-2-inch baking pan with vegetable oil.

In a medium bowl, whisk together the flour, sugar, and salt. In a small saucepan, melt the butter over medium heat. Whisk in the peanut butter and hot water. Bring to a boil over medium-high heat. Simmer for 30 seconds; remove from heat. Let cool for 5 minutes.

In a small bowl, whisk together the buttermilk, egg, baking soda, and vanilla. Add the cooled peanut butter mixture to flour mixture, stirring just until combined. Whisk in the buttermilk mixture until smooth. Stir in the peanuts. Spread the batter in the prepared pan.

Bake until a toothpick inserted in the center comes out clean, 15 to 20 minutes. Let cool slightly in the pan on a wire rack while making frosting.

MAKE THE FROSTING:

In a medium bowl, beat together the peanut butter, melted butter, powdered sugar, and vanilla extract with an electric mixer until smooth.

Spread over the warm bars and sprinkle the peanuts on top. Let cool completely before cutting into 18 bars.

1941

SPECIAL-TREAT GREENS

For a newborn fawn, learning your way around the forest isn't easy. Luckily, Bambi has Thumper there to show him around. Determined to share all the wonders of the forest with the little prince, Thumper shows him the best spots to find greens—reminding him that they are a special treat. These greens are sure to spice up your special occasions, too!

SIDE DISH ✦ GF*, V ✦ YIELD: 4 to 6 servings

Two 9-ounce packages fresh spinach, large stems removed

5 tablespoons butter, divided

⅔ cup fresh breadcrumbs (see note)

1 medium white onion, chopped

3 cloves garlic, minced

1 cup heavy whipping cream

¼ cup plus 2 tablespoons freshly grated Parmesan cheese

¼ teaspoon salt

⅛ teaspoon ground black pepper

In a large pot, cook the spinach in boiling water for 1 minute. Drain well in a colander; cool slightly. Squeeze out excess liquid with your hands and coarsely chop. Set aside.

In a large skillet, melt 3 tablespoons of the butter over medium heat. Add the breadcrumbs. Cook, stirring constantly, until lightly toasted, 1 to 2 minutes. Transfer the crumbs to a plate and set aside.

In the same skillet, melt the remaining 2 tablespoons butter over medium-high heat. Add onion and cook, stirring frequently, until tender, about 2 minutes. Add the garlic and cook, stirring constantly, 1 minute more. Stir in the cream. Bring to boil; simmer for 3 to 5 minutes or until cream starts to thicken.

Stir in ¼ cup cheese, salt, and pepper. Stir just until the cheese is melted. Stir in the chopped spinach. Cook and stir until heated through and sauce is desired consistency.

To serve, top with the toasted breadcrumbs and the remaining 2 tablespoons cheese.

> **NOTE:**
> To make this dish gluten free, use gluten-free breadcrumbs.

1942

CHOCOLATE POT ROAST WITH GREEN GRAVY

Mickey, Donald, and Goofy are hungry! With no food left on their farm, they're worried about how they'll eat. Then Mickey trades their last cow . . . for beans. But they aren't just any beans. They're magical beans, and they lead the three to a land of giants, where the food is bigger and tastier than anything they've ever imagined—including a pot roast (that's very green!) with gravy. This tasty meal inspired by that dish is hearty enough for a giant—or for a few hungry friends to share!

ENTRÉE ✦ GF ✦ YIELD: 8 to 10 servings

FOR THE ROAST

2 teaspoons salt, plus more to taste

½ teaspoon ground black pepper

2 teaspoons unsweetened cocoa powder

1 teaspoon espresso powder

1 teaspoon brown sugar

1 teaspoon ground cumin

½ teaspoon smoked paprika

¼ teaspoon onion powder

One 4-pound top loin roast with fat cap, fat trimmed to ¼ inch

2 tablespoons olive oil

FOR THE GRAVY

½ cup shelled pistachios

2 cups fresh basil leaves

2 cloves garlic, sliced

1 small shallot, chopped

⅓ cup olive oil

1 tablespoon lemon juice

⅓ cup grated Parmesan cheese

¼ cup heavy whipping cream

MAKE THE ROAST:

For the rub, in a small bowl combine 2 teaspoons salt, pepper, cocoa powder, espresso powder, brown sugar, cumin, smoked paprika, and onion powder. Rub the spice mixture all over roast. Place the roast on a plate and refrigerate, uncovered, for at least 4, or up to 24, hours.

Heat the oven to 325°F.

Place a rack inside a roasting pan. In a large skillet, heat the olive oil over medium-high heat. Sear the roast on all sides until browned, about 4 minutes per side. Transfer the roast to the roasting pan, fat-side up. Roast until a meat thermometer registers 120°F to 125°F, about 1 hour (medium doneness).

Transfer to a carving board and cover with foil; let rest for 20 minutes before slicing.

MAKE THE GRAVY:

For green gravy, in a food processor, process the pistachios until coarsely chopped. Add the basil, garlic, and shallot. Process until very finely chopped, stopping to scrape down sides of bowl with a spatula.

Add the olive oil and lemon juice. Process until nearly smooth. Add the Parmesan and cream; process until well combined. Serve with the roast for drizzling over slices.

1947

WILD CHASE TEA BISCUITS

Mr. Toad is always on the go, racing from one place to another. But that doesn't mean he's not willing to stop for a tasty treat. These fabulous biscuits might give him a reason to stop. With such delicious biscuits and homemade strawberry jam, your friends will be sticking around for a while, too!

BREAD ✦ V

YIELD: *2 dozen (2-inch) biscuits and 5 half-pints jam*

FOR THE STRAWBERRY FREEZER JAM

8 cups fresh ripe whole strawberries, hulled, divided

1⅔ cups granulated sugar

5 teaspoons instant powdered fruit pectin

1 tablespoon lemon zest

FOR THE BISCUITS

1½ cups all-purpose flour

½ cup granulated sugar

¼ teaspoon salt

⅛ teaspoon ground cardamom

½ cup cold butter, cut up

1 egg

¼ cup dried currants or chopped dried cherries

1 tablespoon orange zest

Granulated sugar or sparkling sanding sugar (optional)

MAKE THE JAM:

In a large bowl, crush 1 cup of the strawberries with a potato masher. Continue adding berries, 1 cup at a time, crushing them, until you have 4 cups crushed berries.

In a very large bowl, stir together the sugar and fruit pectin. Add the crushed berries and lemon zest. Stir for 3 minutes. Ladle into half-pint freezer containers, leaving ½ inch of headspace at the top. Let stand at room temperature for 30 minutes. Freeze for up to 1 year. Once jam is opened, store in the refrigerator for up to 3 weeks.

MAKE THE BISCUITS:

Heat the oven to 350°F.

In a food processor bowl, combine the flour, sugar, salt, and cardamom. Process until combined. Add the butter pieces. Pulse until the butter is the size of coarse crumbs. Add the egg, currants, and orange zest. Process until combined and dough begins to form a ball in the food processor. If the dough is sticky, wrap in plastic wrap and chill in the refrigerator for 1 to 2 hours.

Line a large rimmed baking pan with parchment paper. On a lightly floured surface, roll the dough out to ¼-inch thickness. Cut out the dough with a round 2-inch biscuit cutter. Place biscuits 1 inch apart on the prepared pan. Sprinkle the tops with additional granulated sugar, if desired.

Bake until bottoms are lightly browned, 8 to 10 minutes. Serve warm with jam.

SLEEPY HOLLOW-EEN PUMPKIN CUPCAKES

Ichabod Crane is a superstitious man, and easily frightened. So it's no wonder that when Ichabod comes across a headless horseman on his journey home from a party, he's terrified. Relive the excitement of that first meeting (but a much less scary version!) with these jack-o'-lantern cupcakes, sure to give any party guest a thrill!

DESSERT ✦ V ✦ YIELD: *24 cupcakes*

FOR THE CUPCAKES

2¼ cups all-purpose flour

1 tablespoon baking powder

1 tablespoon pumpkin pie spice

½ teaspoon baking soda

½ teaspoon salt

½ cup butter, softened

⅔ cup granulated sugar

⅔ cup brown sugar

2 large eggs

1 cup pumpkin puree

¾ cup buttermilk

FOR THE FROSTING

4 ounces cream cheese, room temperature

½ cup butter, softened

2 cups sifted powdered sugar

1 teaspoon orange zest

¼ teaspoon ground cinnamon or pumpkin pie spice

Pinch ground nutmeg (optional)

Orange gel paste food coloring

12 pretzel sticks

2 ounces bittersweet chocolate, broken or cut into small pieces

MAKE THE CUPCAKES:

Heat the oven to 350°F. Line 24 standard muffin cups with paper liners.

In a medium bowl, whisk together the flour, baking powder, pumpkin pie spice, baking soda, and salt; set aside. In a large bowl, beat the butter with an electric mixer for 30 seconds. Add the granulated sugar and brown sugar. Beat on medium-high until fluffy, about 3 minutes, scraping down sides of bowl with a rubber spatula as needed. Add the eggs and beat until well combined, about 2 minutes. Add the pumpkin and buttermilk. Beat until combined. Add the flour mixture and beat on low just until combined. Spoon the batter into the lined muffin cups, filling each about two-thirds full.

Bake until a toothpick inserted into center comes out clean, 15 to 20 minutes. Remove cupcakes from pan and cool completely on a wire rack.

MAKE THE FROSTING:

In a large bowl, beat the cream cheese and butter with an electric mixer until well combined. Gradually beat in the powdered sugar. Beat in the orange zest, cinnamon, nutmeg, and enough orange food coloring to achieve desired color. Place in a decorating bag fitted with a large star tip. Pipe icing onto cupcakes in lines to look the texture of a pumpkin.

Break the pretzel sticks in half and insert a pretzel piece into the top edge of each cupcake top for a stem. Decorate the cupcakes with the chocolate to look like jack-o'-lantern faces.

1949

CHAPTER 2

1950–1969

In the late 1940s, with the war over and his animators returning home, Walt Disney refocused his attention to feature films, releasing the hugely successful film *Cinderella* in 1950. This whimsical retelling of the classic Perrault fairy tale was so popular that it helped fund the production of multiple new projects and animated films over the next decade. Among these films was 1953's *Peter Pan*, a now-beloved classic that stands out as the last film that all of Disney's group of animators known as the "Nine Old Men" worked on together. Peter Pan's spunky sidekick, Tinker Bell, has become one of Disney's most iconic characters, spawning her own franchise of films and television appearances.

Peter Pan was far from the only lasting film released by Disney during the '50s and '60s. Such enduring classics as *Alice in Wonderland* (1951), *Lady and the Tramp* (1953), *Sleeping Beauty* (1959), *One Hundred and One Dalmatians* (1961), *The Sword in the Stone* (1963), and *The Jungle Book* (1967) also made their debuts during this era. Perennial favorites, these films have enchanted children and adults around the world ever since. But, while producing these earlier films, Walt Disney—ever the dreamer—shifted his focus to a goal much bigger than animated films: the creation of a family-focused theme park in California!

From the get-go, Disney intended the park to be a small place for families, where there was fun for every member, no matter their age. In fact, one of Walt's initial plans called for only eight acres of land to be used across the street from the Disney studio in Burbank. But as ideas for the park grew, it soon became clear that more space would be needed to fulfill Walt's vision. In the early 1950s, the Company purchased approximately 160 acres of land in Anaheim, California, and in 1954, construction began on what had begun to be called "Disneyland."

On July 17, 1955—less than a year after construction began—the press got its first peek at the exciting new park. The event was aired nationally on television to an estimated 90 million viewers, which only fueled the excitement of the public. Disneyland opened to the public the following day and featured dozens of rides and exhibits spread across five lands: Adventureland, Fantasyland, Frontierland, Main Street, U.S.A., and Tomorrowland. The price of admission for an adult was only $1. Factoring in inflation, that amounts to not much more than $11 today!

The park was an instant success, and the Company was sailing high, with a proud Walt Disney at the helm. However, a little more than a decade later, in 1966, Walt Disney passed away, leaving the future of his company and its legacy up in the air.

MOUSE-APPROVED CHEESY CORN PUFFS

Cinderella starts almost every morning scattering corn in the yard for the animals. For the chickens, it's just breakfast, but for Cinderella's mouse friend Gus, it's a special treat—a fact he makes known by gathering up as many kernels as his little arms can carry! This irresistible cheesy corn puff would make a treat even more special for Gus.

APPETIZER/SNACK ✦ V ✦ YIELD: about 4 dozen puffs

1 cup water

¼ cup butter

½ teaspoon salt

Pinch cayenne pepper

1 cup all-purpose flour

4 large eggs

1 cup shredded sharp cheddar cheese

¼ cup fresh or frozen corn kernels, thawed

¼ cup grated Parmesan cheese

1 tablespoon yellow cornmeal

Heat the oven to 425°F. Adjust the racks to the center of oven. Line two large baking sheets with parchment paper.

In a large saucepan, bring the water, butter, salt, and cayenne to a boil over medium heat. Add the flour all at once. Stir with a wooden spoon until a smooth ball forms. Remove from heat and let stand for 5 minutes. Add the eggs, one at a time, beating with an electric mixer after each addition until smooth. Stir in the cheddar cheese and corn.

Using two spoons or a small cookie scoop, drop dough into 1-inch balls, 1 inch apart, on the prepared baking sheets. Sprinkle the tops of the balls with the Parmesan cheese and cornmeal.

Bake until golden brown, 20 to 25 minutes. Serve warm.

1950

BIBBIDI-BOBBIDI BLUEBERRY TARTS

Bibbidi-Bobbidi-Boo! With those three words and a wave of her Fairy Godmother's wand, Cinderella knows something wonderful will happen! But her Fairy Godmother can't always be around, so Cinderella has found lots of other ways to make something plain into something magical. These bibbidi-bobbidi-blueberry tarts remind us that the Fairy Godmother is always watching over Cinderella, even when they can't be together.

DESSERT ✦ V ✦ YIELD: 12 tarts

FOR THE TARTS

1 cup finely ground sugar cookie crumbs

2 tablespoons unsalted butter, melted

Two 8-ounce packages cream cheese, softened

⅓ cup granulated sugar

⅓ cup sour cream

3 tablespoons wild blueberry powder

1 teaspoon lemon zest

2 large eggs, lightly beaten

Purple food coloring (optional)

FOR THE BLUEBERRY SAUCE

¼ cup granulated sugar

2 teaspoons cornstarch

⅓ cup water

1 cup fresh blueberries

FOR SERVING

Fresh mint leaves

Lemon peel (optional)

MAKE THE TARTS:

Heat the oven to 325°F.

Line 12 standard muffin cups with foil liners; set aside. In a medium bowl, stir together the cookie crumbs and melted butter. Divide evenly among the muffin cups. Press the crumbs lightly with the back of a spoon to compact the crusts evenly into the bottoms of the liners. Bake for 5 minutes.

In a large bowl, beat the cream cheese with an electric mixer on medium for 1 minute. Add the sugar and beat until well combined. Beat in the sour cream, blueberry powder, food coloring (if using), and lemon zest. Add the eggs one at a time, beating just until combined after each. Spoon the cream cheese mixture evenly over the crusts in muffin cups. Bake until set, 15 to 20 minutes.

Cool the tarts in the pan on a wire rack for 30 minutes. Remove tarts from the pan and chill 3 to 4 hours. If storing overnight, allow to cool completely, then refrigerate in an airtight container.

MAKE THE BLUEBERRY SAUCE:

In a small saucepan, combine the sugar and cornstarch. Add the water and blueberries. Cook and stir over medium heat until bubbly. Transfer to a bowl and cool completely.

To serve, peel the foil from tarts. Spoon blueberry sauce over each tart. Garnish with mint leaves and/or lemon peel.

QUEEN OF HEARTS JAM TARTS

The Queen of Hearts is particular. She likes things to be a certain way—*her* way! And that means lots of red everywhere you look. Luckily, these delicious jam tarts fit the bill. Perfect for a light snack—or even a tea party—these are sure to leave even someone as particular as the Queen of Hearts begging for more. Just don't run out, or it's off with your head!

DESSERT ✦ V ✦ YIELD: *9 tarts*

FOR THE POWDERED SUGAR ICING

1 cup sifted powdered sugar

1 tablespoon milk, plus more as desired

Dash almond extract

FOR THE TARTS

2 cups all-purpose flour

2 teaspoons granulated sugar

½ teaspoon salt

½ cup cold unsalted butter, cut up

4 to 5 tablespoons cold water

¼ teaspoon almond extract (optional)

⅔ cup tart cherry preserves

1 egg yolk

1 tablespoon water

Coarse sanding sugar

MAKE THE POWDERED SUGAR ICING:

In a small bowl, stir together sifted powdered sugar, milk, and almond extract. Stir in enough additional milk to make desired consistency. Set aside.

MAKE THE TARTS:

In a large bowl, combine the flour, granulated sugar, and salt. Cut in the butter with a pastry cutter or two knives until the butter is the size of small peas. Gradually add 4 tablespoons water, mixing with a fork, until the mixture is evenly moistened. Add just enough additional water to make a dough that holds together. Shape the dough into a ball and divide it in half. Flatten each half into a square. Wrap with plastic wrap and chill in the refrigerator for 1 hour.

Place one portion of dough on a lightly floured surface. Roll to an 8-by-10-inch rectangle. Cut the dough into 9 rectangles using a fluted pastry wheel or sharp knife. Transfer to a parchment-lined baking pan. If using almond extract, place cherry preserves in a small bowl; stir extract into the preserves. Spoon 1 tablespoon of preserves into the center of each dough rectangle.

Place the remaining dough portion onto the lightly floured surface. Roll out the dough to an 8-by-10-inch rectangle. Cut the dough into 9 rectangles as before. Use a small 1-inch heart-shaped cookie cutter to cut a heart shape from center of each dough rectangle.

In a small bowl, whisk together the egg yolk and water. Brush the egg mixture on the edges of the pastry rectangles on baking sheet. Place a cutout dough rectangle on top of each cherry-topped pastry. Press the edges lightly to seal. Brush the tops with more egg mixture and sprinkle with sanding sugar.

Bake until golden brown, 15 to 20 minutes. Serve warm or at room temperature. If desired, drizzle with powdered sugar icing.

1951

CHESHIRE CAT GRIN

Nothing in Wonderland is quite as it seems, and that is most apparent with the mysterious Cheshire Cat, who has a tendency to leave his smile behind when he vanishes! This color-changing libation won't make you grow bigger or smaller, but it is sure to leave a grin on your face long after it's gone!

DRINK ✦ GF, V, V+ ✦ YIELD: 2 drinks

FOR THE SYRUP

1 cup water

1 cup raw (demerara) sugar

1 teaspoon butterfly pea flower powder

FOR THE ICE CUBES

¼ cup lavender blossoms or other edible flowers

¾ cup fresh lemon juice, strained

FOR SERVING

8 ounces (4 ounces per glass) lemon-flavored sparkling water, chilled

1½ ounces fresh lemon juice

Lavender sprigs, for garnish

MAKE THE SYRUP:

In a small saucepan, heat the water and sugar over medium heat, stirring often, until the mixture begins to simmer and the sugar is dissolved. Remove from heat. Stir in the pea powder; cover and let steep for 20 minutes. Strain into a glass jar and cool completely.

MAKE THE ICE CUBES:

Sprinkle the lavender blossoms into enough ice cube trays to make 2 drinks (about 4 standard cubes). Pour the strained lemon juice over the blossoms. Freeze for 4 hours or overnight.

To serve, place ¾ ounce of the blue syrup in each of two 8-ounce cocktail glasses. Add sparkling water to each glass. Do not stir. Add ¾ ounce lemon juice to each glass. Add 2 lemon ice cubes to each glass. Garnish with lavender sprigs.

Wait for the magic color change from blue to purple!

1951

TICK-TOCK CROC DRINK

If there's one thing Captain Hook fears, it's the crocodile! Luckily, he can always tell the croc is coming by the sound of a clock tick-tocking in its belly. One tick-tock and you'll be running, too . . . to get another one of these delicious green beverages!

DRINK ✦ GF, V, V+ ✦ YIELD: 2 drinks

FOR THE JALAPEÑO SYRUP

½ cup raw (demerara) sugar

½ cup water

1 jalapeño, sliced (seeded if desired)

FOR THE MINT SUGAR

¼ cup granulated sugar

¼ cup fresh mint leaves

FOR SERVING

4 tablespoons Granny Smith green apple beverage syrup

Crushed ice

1 cup apple juice, chilled

One 7.2-ounce can club soda, chilled

2 lemon wedges

2 very thin green apple slices, for garnish (optional)

MAKE THE JALAPEÑO SYRUP:

In a small saucepan, combine the raw sugar, water, and jalapeño. Bring just to a simmer over medium heat, stirring frequently to dissolve the sugar. Remove from heat. Cover and let steep for 20 minutes. Strain into a glass jar; cool completely. Reserve jalapeño slices, if desired.

MAKE THE MINT SUGAR:

In a small food processor or bullet-style blender, combine the granulated sugar and mint leaves. Process until the mint is ground and sugar is greenish in color. Right before serving the drink, spread the mint sugar onto a small plate or saucer.

To serve, brush the rim of 2 margarita glasses with some of the jalapeño syrup (or the green apple syrup for less bite). Dip the glass rims into the mint sugar, getting as much sugar to stick as possible. Fill each glass half full with crushed ice. Pour 1 tablespoon jalapeño syrup and 2 tablespoons Granny Smith apple syrup into each glass. Top with apple juice and club soda. Squeeze lemon wedges into each drink and drop into the glasses.

If desired, garnish each drink with a candied jalapeño slice and very thin apple slice.

1953

CRISPY OVEN-FRIED CODFISH

Captain Hook has always been after Peter Pan. But when the two face off in battle once more, it's Peter who gets the upper hand. Hook's only way out is to admit defeat— by declaring himself a codfish! Enjoy this Captain Hook-inspired meal alongside a tasty homemade tartar sauce!

ENTRÉE ✦ GF* ✦ YIELD: 4 servings

FOR THE FISH

Four 4- to 6-ounce fresh or frozen cod fillets, ¾-inch thick, thawed if frozen

½ cup panko breadcrumbs

¼ cup grated Parmesan cheese

2 teaspoons finely chopped fresh dill or ½ teaspoon dried dillweed

¼ teaspoon salt

¼ teaspoon ground black pepper

⅓ cup whole milk

½ cup all-purpose flour

2 tablespoons olive oil, divided

FOR THE TARTAR SAUCE

1 cup mayonnaise

⅓ cup chopped dill or sweet pickles

1 tablespoon pickle juice

2 teaspoons fresh lemon juice

1 tablespoon drained capers, finely chopped

FOR SERVING

4 lemon wedges

MAKE THE FISH:

Heat the oven to 450°F.

Place an extra-large cast-iron skillet (or other ovenproof skillet) in the oven for 5 to 10 minutes while preparing the fish. Pat the fish fillets dry with paper towels; set aside.

In a shallow dish, combine the breadcrumbs, Parmesan cheese, dill, salt, and pepper. In two other shallow dishes, place the milk and flour.

Remove the skillet from oven and drizzle with 1 tablespoon of the olive oil, rotating the skillet to coat. Dip the fish pieces in the milk, then in the flour. Dip again in the milk, then the breadcrumb mixture. Place the fish in the hot skillet. Drizzle the fish pieces with the remaining 1 tablespoon olive oil. Return the skillet to the oven.

Bake until the fish flakes easily with a fork, 6 to 8 minutes.

MAKE THE TARTAR SAUCE:

In a small bowl, stir together the mayonnaise, chopped pickle, pickle juice, lemon juice, and capers.

Serve the fish with tartar sauce and lemon wedges.

> **NOTE:**
> To make this dish gluten free, use gluten-free panko breadcrumbs.

1953

GOOD-DOGGIE DOUGHNUTS

Life with Darling and Jim Dear is everything Lady dreamed it would be. Each morning she gets the newspaper, greets Jim Dear, and enjoys a tasty breakfast of coffee and doughnuts. Replicate Lady's breakfast for the pooches in your own life with this dog-friendly doughnut recipe sure to leave them begging for more!

DESSERT (FOR YOUR CANINE COMPANIONS!) ✦ V
YIELD: About 4 dozen dog treats

2 large eggs, beaten

⅔ cup natural peanut butter

⅔ cup natural applesauce

2 tablespoons honey

2 tablespoons vegetable oil

2 cups whole wheat flour

1 cup quick rolled oats

Heat the oven to 300°F. Line 2 large rimmed baking pans with parchment paper.

In a large bowl, combine the eggs, peanut butter, applesauce, honey, oil, flour, and oats. Stir with a wooden spoon until well combined, adding a little more flour if the dough is sticky.

For each doughnut, scoop about 2 tablespoons of dough onto a lightly floured surface. Roll into a 4-inch log. Bend each log into a doughnut shape and press ends together to seal and make a ring shape. Repeat with the remaining dough, placing doughnuts 1 inch apart on the prepared baking sheets.

Bake until golden brown, about 20 minutes. Let cool on the sheets for 5 minutes. Transfer to a wire rack to cool completely.

Store in an airtight container in the refrigerator for up to 2 weeks.

1955

VERY TALL BUTTERCREAM BIRTHDAY CAKE

It's Briar Rose's sixteenth birthday, and the Three Good Fairies are determined to celebrate. But making a cake without magic isn't as easy as it seems! Luckily for Fauna, she's got her wand at the ready. A single flick and the ingredients get to work on their own, making a gorgeous cake just in time for the big birthday celebration.

DESSERT ✦ V ✦ YIELD: 12 to 16 servings

> **NOTE:**
> You will need to prepare this cake recipe twice to make 4 layers for the very tall cake.

FOR THE CAKE

Vegetable oil, for greasing pans

2⅓ cups sifted cake flour

1 tablespoon baking powder

¼ teaspoon fine sea salt

10 tablespoons unsalted butter, room temperature

1⅓ cups granulated sugar

4 large egg whites, room temperature

1 cup whole milk

1 teaspoon vanilla extract

MAKE THE CAKE:

Heat the oven to 325°F. Grease two 6-by-2-inch round cake pans. Line the bottom of each pan with a circle of parchment paper cut to size. Grease the parchment paper with vegetable oil and flour the pans, tapping out excess flour.

In a medium bowl, whisk together the cake flour, baking powder, and salt. In a large bowl, beat the butter with an electric mixer on medium-high for 30 seconds.

Gradually beat in the sugar until fluffy, about 5 minutes. Beat in the egg whites, one at a time, beating well after each addition. Alternately add the flour mixture and milk, about one-third at a time, beating after each addition. Scrape the sides of the bowl with a rubber spatula as needed. Stir in the vanilla. Divide the batter evenly between the prepared cake pans.

Bake until a toothpick inserted comes out clean, 35 to 40 minutes. Cool in the pans on a wire rack for 10 minutes. Remove the cakes from the pans and cool completely on the rack. Wash pans and repeat the recipe to make 4 layers.

continued on page 69

1959

continued from 66

FOR THE BUTTERCREAM FROSTING

4 cups unsalted butter, room temperature

Two 14-ounce cans sweetened condensed milk

½ teaspoon fine sea salt

1 teaspoon clear vanilla extract

Blue gel paste food coloring

Yellow gel paste food coloring

MAKE THE BUTTERCREAM FROSTING:

In the bowl of a stand mixer fitted with the whisk attachment, whip the butter on medium-high until very light and whiter in color, about 5 minutes.

Gradually beat in the sweetened condensed milk, adding it about one-third at a time, beating well after each addition. Beat in the salt and vanilla extract. Scrape down the whisk attachment and switch to the paddle attachment.

Slowly mix the buttercream with the paddle attachment for about 3 minutes to remove the large air pockets. (Frosting should be smooth and creamy.) Remove 3 cups of the frosting. Place 2 cups in one bowl and 1 cup in another bowl. Stir in desired amount of blue food coloring into the 2 cups frosting. Stir desired amount of yellow food coloring into the 1 cup frosting. Place blue frosting in a disposable piping bag fitted with a medium round tip. Place yellow frosting in a disposable piping bag fitted with a medium star tip; set aside.

To assemble and frost cake, use a large serrated knife to level the tops of all cake layers. Spread a thin layer of white icing over the tops and sides of all four cake layers. Place one cake layer on a cake plate. Pipe about ¼ cup blue frosting over the cake layer and spread to edges. Pipe round balls around the bottom of the cake layer and squiggles around the top of it for drips. Place the second layer slightly askew on top. Repeat piping ¼ cup blue frosting over the cake layer and spreading to edges. Repeat piping squiggles for drips. Repeat with remaining layers.

To stabilize the cake, insert 3 or 4 wooden skewers down through all cake layers. Trim skewers with kitchen shears to be level with the cake top. Use a long metal spatula to make the frosting smooth on the top where the skewers went in. Pipe rosettes and cording with yellow frosting on top layer as desired.

Don't forget to remove the skewers as you cut the cake to serve.

SLEEPY CHAMOMILE TEA LATTE

When Aurora pricks her finger on the spindle, she falls into a deep sleep—one that can only be broken by true love's kiss. Get your own restful night's sleep with this soothing chamomile tea—sure to send you to bed happy, but able to wake up in the morning!

DRINK ✦ GF, V, V+* ✦ YIELD: 2 lattes

2 cinnamon sticks

4 whole cloves

One 3-inch strip lemon peel

1 slice fresh gingerroot

1½ cups water

3 tablespoons loose-leaf chamomile flowers or 3 chamomile tea bags

1 cup whole milk

½ teaspoon vanilla extract

1 to 2 tablespoons honey

Ground cinnamon and/or ground ginger, for garnish

In a medium saucepan, combine the cinnamon, cloves, lemon peel, gingerroot, and water. Bring to a simmer over medium heat. Reduce the heat to low and simmer gently for 5 minutes. Remove from heat and add the chamomile tea. Cover and let steep for 10 minutes.

Meanwhile, in a small saucepan, heat the milk and vanilla over medium heat. While heating the milk, whisk it briskly with a wire whisk or a milk frothing wand. When warm, remove from heat.

When the tea is done steeping, strain through a fine-mesh strainer into a teapot or directly into two large teacups or mugs. Stir in the honey and milk, leaving any froth behind. Spoon the milk froth over the tops of each cup. Sprinkle with ground cinnamon and/or ground ginger.

NOTE:
To make this drink vegan, use a barista-blend oat milk instead of whole milk. (If you also need it to be gluten free, be sure it does not contain gluten.)

1959

TOWERING ROAST BEEF SANDWICHES

Watching over 99 puppies is hungry work! It's no wonder that Horace makes himself a big sandwich for dinner! Filled to the brim with roast beef, lettuce, and cheese, it's a treat that even the most determined crook couldn't resist stopping to take a bite of. For a bit of an added kick, top off the sandwich with a little "Horace-radish"!

ENTRÉE ✦ YIELD: 4 large sandwiches (8 servings)

FOR THE HOMEMADE BUTTERMILK WHITE BREAD

One 0.25-ounce package active dry yeast

¼ cup warm water (110°F)

2 cups buttermilk

2 tablespoons granulated sugar

1½ teaspoons salt

1 tablespoon butter

5½ to 6 cups all-purpose flour, divided

Vegetable oil, for greasing

MAKE THE HOMEMADE BUTTERMILK WHITE BREAD:

In a small dish, combine the yeast and warm water. Let stand for 5 minutes to dissolve the yeast.

In a medium saucepan, heat the buttermilk, sugar, salt, and butter over medium-low heat to 110°F to 115°F, stirring frequently. Remove from heat.

In a large bowl, combine 2 cups of the flour, the buttermilk mixture, and yeast mixture. Beat with an electric mixer on medium to combine, scraping the bowl as needed. Beat on high speed for 3 minutes. Stir in enough of the remaining flour with a wooden spoon to make a soft dough that can be shaped into a ball.

Turn the dough out onto a lightly floured surface. Knead, working in additional flour, until the dough is moderately stiff, smooth, and elastic, about 6 minutes.

continued on page 74

1961

continued from 73

FOR THE SANDWICH

1 loaf Homemade Buttermilk White Bread (page 73) or bakery cottage bread, unsliced

⅓ cup mayonnaise

2 tablespoons sour cream

2 tablespoons prepared horseradish

¼ teaspoon ground black pepper

4 red or green leaf lettuce leaves, or 8 Bibb lettuce leaves

2 pounds thinly sliced medium-rare deli roast beef

4 ounces white cheddar cheese, thinly sliced

2 medium tomatoes, thickly sliced

Transfer the dough to a large lightly oiled bowl, turning to coat the dough on both sides. Cover with a clean cotton kitchen towel or plastic wrap. Let rise in a warm place until doubled in size, about 1 hour.

Press down the dough to release large air bubbles. Turn the dough out onto a lightly floured surface. Let rest for 10 minutes.

Grease a 9-by-5-by-3-inch loaf pan. Shape dough into a loaf by folding in the sides and gently rolling into a log. Place it seam-side down in the greased pan. Cover and let rise in a warm place until nearly doubled in size, about 30 minutes.

Heat the oven to 375°F. Bake until the bread sounds hollow when tapped, 40 to 45 minutes. If necessary, cover with foil the last 15 minutes of baking to prevent overbrowning.

Let cool in the pan on a wire rack for 5 minutes. Remove the bread from the pan and cool completely on the rack.

MAKE THE SANDWICH:

Cut eight ¾-inch-thick slices from the homemade buttermilk white bread loaf.

In a small bowl, stir together the mayonnaise, sour cream, horseradish, and pepper. Spread each slice of bread with about 1 tablespoon of sauce.

Layer the lettuce, roast beef, cheese, and tomatoes on top of 4 of the slices. Top with the remaining bread slices. Use long toothpicks to skewer each side of the tall sandwiches before cutting in half with a serrated knife.

DISAPPEARING WIZARD MIX

A battle between two wizards is a sight to see, but even the fiercest battle needs to follow some rules! Flying on a broom is fine. Turning Arthur into a fish is fine. But both Merlin and Madam Mim agree: There will be "no disappearing!" The same can't be said of this magical mix. Made of wizard hats, wands, and fish, it's sure to disappear by the handful!

APPETIZER/SNACK ✦ V ✦ YIELD: 16 cups

3 cups square rice cereal

3 cups bugle-shaped snack crackers

2 cups square white cheddar crackers

3 cups fish-shaped cheese crackers

2 cups pretzel sticks

1 cup sesame stick crackers

1 cup roasted cashews

½ cup pepitas

½ cup butter

2 tablespoons olive oil

1 tablespoon soy sauce

Few dashes bottled hot pepper sauce (optional)

2 tablespoons brown sugar

1½ teaspoons smoked paprika

1 teaspoon garlic powder

1 teaspoon salt

1 cup wasabi peas or corn nuts

Heat the oven to 300°F.

In a very large roasting pan, combine the rice cereal, bugle-shaped crackers, white cheddar crackers, fish crackers, pretzels, sesame sticks, cashews, and pepitas. Bake for 5 minutes.

In a small saucepan, combine the butter, olive oil, soy sauce, hot sauce (if using), brown sugar, paprika, garlic powder, and salt. Cook over medium heat, stirring constantly, until just simmering and the brown sugar is dissolved. Pour over the warm cracker mixture in the pan. Thoroughly toss the mixture until evenly coated. Return to the oven and bake for 1 hour, stirring every 15 minutes.

When done baking, stir in the wasabi peas and toss to coat the peas.

Serve warm or at room temperature. Store at room temperature in an airtight container for up to 2 weeks (cool completely before storing).

1963

77

BARE NECESSITIES BANANA MUFFINS

In the jungle, there's no lack of fresh fruit. And when it comes to fruit, it's bananas for Baloo and Mowgli. Cooked up in a nice, warm muffin, these make a perfect breakfast before a lazy day of floating down the river!

BREAD ✦ V ✦ YIELD: 12 muffins

FOR THE STREUSEL

3 tablespoons granulated sugar

3 tablespoons brown sugar

3 tablespoons all-purpose flour

Dash salt

2 tablespoons unsalted butter, melted

2 tablespoons chopped walnuts

FOR THE MUFFINS

Nonstick cooking spray

2 cups all-purpose flour

1 cup whole wheat flour

2 teaspoons baking powder

½ teaspoon baking soda

½ teaspoon salt

¾ cup granulated sugar

2 large eggs

6 tablespoons unsalted butter, melted

1¼ cups buttermilk

1 ripe banana, mashed

1 teaspoon vanilla extract

½ cup chopped walnuts, toasted

Heat the oven to 375°F. Spray a standard 12-cup muffin tin generously with nonstick cooking spray, spraying the top as well as the cups; set aside.

MAKE THE STREUSEL:

In a small bowl, combine the granulated sugar, brown sugar, flour, and salt. Stir in the butter and walnuts; set aside.

MAKE THE MUFFINS:

In a large bowl, stir together the all-purpose flour, whole wheat flour, baking powder, baking soda, salt, and sugar. In a medium bowl, beat the eggs. Whisk in the melted butter, buttermilk, banana, and vanilla.

Add the banana mixture to the flour mixture. Fold together gently with a rubber spatula until nearly combined. Stir in the ½ cup walnuts just until combined. (Do not overmix.) Divide the batter evenly among the muffin cups. Sprinkle the streusel over top of the batter.

Bake until golden brown and a toothpick inserted into center comes out clean, 20 to 25 minutes. Cool in the pan for 5 minutes. Remove from the pan and serve warm.

NOTE:
These muffins will be large and have tops that spread out onto the top of the muffin pan. Use a knife or fork if necessary to remove muffins from the pan without breaking tops.

1967

CHAPTER 3

1970-1989

The 1970s and 1980s were a time of transition for Walt Disney Productions. With its founder gone, the studio released fewer animated films than before. However, all was not lost. Following some of the projects initiated but left behind by Walt, such classics as *The Aristocats* (1970), *Robin Hood* (1973), *The Many Adventures of Winnie the Pooh* (1977), and *The Fox and the Hound* (1981) joined Disney's cinematic canon. These films have become beloved family favorites and are shared across generations among grandparents, parents, and children.

But the 1970s and 1980s focused on more than just filmmaking. Prior to his death, Walt Disney purchased more than 27,000 acres of land near Orlando, Florida. Building off the success of Disneyland, his vision was to create not a single theme park, but an entire world in which families could escape everyday life and enjoy quality time together. Construction on the eventual Walt Disney World Resort began in 1967 with the creation of a 200-acre lake to be known as the Seven Seas Lagoon, an 18-hole golf course, two hotels, and the park itself. Known as the Magic Kingdom, the park contained six unique lands: Main Street, U.S.A., Tomorrowland, Fantasyland, Frontierland, Liberty Square, and Adventureland. The heart of the park is the breathtaking Cinderella Castle, which took 18 months to build and stands an impressive 189 feet tall.

Walt Disney World opened to the public on October 1, 1971, but it continues to add elements to this day. In 1973, Tom Sawyer Island and the Pirates of the Caribbean attraction made their debut. Space Mountain and the Carousel of Progress followed in 1975 and Big Thunder Mountain Railroad in 1980. Then, on October 1, 1982, EPCOT Center (today known as EPCOT) opened. It initially featured five Future World pavilions and nine World Showcase pavilions, which offered a variety of cuisines for guests to try from all around the globe: Mexico, China, Germany, Italy, The American Adventure, Japan, France, United Kingdom, and Canada.

In 1984, new leadership was brought in. Walt Disney Productions' new chairman and CEO Michael D. Eisner and president Frank G. Wells enacted a bold new creative vision to help steer Walt Disney Productions into the future.

ROQUEFORT BLUE CHEESE WHEELS

As Madame Bonfamille's pets, Marie, Toulouse, and Berlioz have access to the finest foods. And what could be better than sharing a delicious little treat with their good friend Roquefort the Mouse? Cooked up in a puff pastry, this treat is a snack worthy of any Aristocat!

APPETIZER/SNACK ✦ V ✦ YIELD: About 36 pinwheels

4 ounces Roquefort cheese, room temperature

4 ounces cream cheese, room temperature

1 large egg

¼ cup finely chopped green onion

1 teaspoon finely chopped fresh rosemary

½ teaspoon cracked black pepper

Half of one 17.3-ounce package frozen puff pastry, thawed (1 sheet)

1 cup toasted pecans, finely chopped

1 egg yolk, beaten

In a medium bowl, combine the Roquefort and cream cheese. Beat with an electric mixer until combined. Beat in the egg. With a rubber spatula, stir in the green onion, rosemary, and pepper.

On a lightly floured work surface, unfold the pastry and roll out to a 10-by-12-inch rectangle. Spread the cheese mixture evenly over the pastry, leaving a 1-inch border along one of the long edges. Sprinkle the pecans evenly over the cheese mixture.

Brush the egg yolk over the 1-inch strip of pastry without filling. Starting at the opposite edge, roll up the pastry tightly into a spiral log. Seal the edge to the log by pressing and pinching. Wrap the log with plastic wrap and chill in the refrigerator for 1 to 2 hours or until very firm.

Heat the oven to 400°F. Line a large rimmed baking pan with parchment paper; set aside.

Place the chilled log on a cutting board. Cut with a sharp knife into ¼-inch-thick slices. Place slices 1 inch apart on the prepared baking sheet.

Bake until golden brown and crispy, 15 to 20 minutes. Serve warm or at room temperature.

1970

COIN COOKIES

Robin Hood is known throughout Nottingham for one thing: taking from the rich and giving to the poor. And there's nothing he likes more than taking gold coins from Prince John and his sidekick Sir Hiss. Inspired by the gold coins in Prince John's treasure chest, these coin cookies are one treat you won't want to share!

DESSERT ✦ V ✦ YIELD: About 4 dozen cookies

¾ cup butter, softened

1 cup granulated sugar

½ teaspoon baking powder

½ teaspoon salt

1 large egg

1 teaspoon vanilla extract

2½ cups all-purpose flour

¼ cup fine yellow cornmeal

2 teaspoons lemon zest

Fine sanding sugar, yellow or gold

Edible gold luster dust and 2 teaspoons vodka (optional)

In a large mixing bowl, beat the butter with an electric mixer on medium-high for 30 seconds. Add the sugar, baking powder, and salt. Beat on medium-high until fluffy, about 3 minutes, scraping the sides of the bowl with a rubber spatula as needed. Beat in the egg and vanilla until combined. Gradually beat in the flour on low. Beat in the cornmeal and lemon zest until combined.

Divide the dough in half. Shape each half into a 7-inch log. Wrap the logs in plastic wrap. Chill in the refrigerator for at least 2, or up to 24, hours. If the dough is soft, reshape the logs every 30 minutes during chilling so they keep a round shape.

Heat the oven to 375°F. Line a cookie sheet with parchment paper.

Place one log on a cutting board. Use a sharp knife to cut it into ¼-inch-thick slices. Place the slices 1 inch apart on the prepared cookie sheet. Sprinkle the tops with sanding sugar. Bake until the edges are lightly browned, 6 to 8 minutes. Transfer to a wire rack to cool. Repeat with the remaining log.

In a tiny bowl, stir together ½ teaspoon gold luster dust and the vodka. Brush on edges of baked cookies. Let dry for a few minutes.

1973

SMACKEREL OF HONEYCAKES

Winnie the Pooh is always on the hunt for honey . . . and he's not afraid to go right to the source: the beehive. But pretending to be a rain cloud isn't as easy as it seems, and poor Pooh finds that it's not the best way to secure a smackerel of honey. These sweet honeycakes decorated with bees are sure to satisfy any craving for honey . . . without the danger of sticking your paw in a hive!

DESSERT ✦ V ✦ YIELD: 12 honeycakes

FOR THE CUPCAKES

2¼ cups all-purpose flour

2 teaspoons baking powder

1 teaspoon salt

¾ cup unsalted butter, softened

¾ cup granulated sugar

⅓ cup honey

1 teaspoon vanilla extract

2 large eggs plus 1 egg yolk, room temperature

¾ cup buttermilk

MAKE THE CUPCAKES:

Heat the oven to 350°F.

Line 12 standard muffin cups with paper liners; set aside.

In a medium bowl, whisk together the flour, baking powder, and salt. In a large mixing bowl, beat the softened butter on medium-high for 30 seconds. Gradually beat in the granulated sugar until light and fluffy, scraping the sides of the bowl with a rubber spatula as needed, 4 to 5 minutes. Beat in the honey and vanilla extract. Beat in the eggs and egg yolk, one at a time, beating well after each addition. With the mixer on low, add the flour mixture and buttermilk alternately, adding about one-third at a time. Beat just until combined.

Scoop or spoon the batter into the prepared muffin cups. Bake until a toothpick inserted in the center comes out clean, 15 to 20 minutes. Cool in the pan for 5 minutes; transfer to a wire rack to cool slightly while you make the glaze.

continued on page 88

1977

continued from 87

FOR THE GLAZE

¼ cup honey

2 tablespoons brown sugar

2 tablespoons unsalted butter

FOR THE FONDANT HONEYBEES

Yellow fondant

Black edible marker

24 almond slices

FOR DECORATING

1 cup buttercream frosting (page 69), or store-bought frosting

Yellow food coloring

MAKE THE GLAZE:

In a small saucepan, combine the honey, brown sugar, and butter. Bring the mixture just to a simmer over medium-low heat. Turn off the heat but keep warm on the burner.

Spoon the glaze slowly over the warm cupcakes on the wire rack, allowing it all to soak in. Cool the cupcakes completely.

MAKE THE FONDANT HONEYBEES:

Use the purchased yellow fondant to shape by hand ½-inch oval bee bodies. Paint stripes on the bee bodies using a black edible marker. Insert 2 almond slices into each bee for wings.

DECORATE THE CAKES:

Tint the buttercream frosting light yellow with food coloring: Start with a single drop, stir to incorporate, then add additional drops, stirring after each addition until desired color is achieved. Place in a disposable piping bag with a large round tip. Pipe a 1-inch beehive on top of each cupcake. Add a fondant honeybee to each cupcake.

BLUSTERY DAY CARROT SOUP

Winnie the Pooh's good friend Rabbit meticulously cares for *all* the vegetables growing in his garden, but the carrots are his favorite. But what can one do with a healthy harvest of carrots? Turn them into a delicious soup, perfect for sharing with friends on a cold, blustery day, of course!

APPETIZER ✦ GF, V ✦ YIELD: 4 to 6 servings

1 small bulb fennel with tops

3 tablespoons butter

6 large carrots, peeled and coarsely chopped

2 small onions, chopped

2 cups chicken or vegetable broth, plus more if needed

2 cups water

2 teaspoons grated fresh gingerroot

2 large strips orange peel

½ teaspoon salt

¼ teaspoon ground black pepper

Sour cream or plain yogurt, for garnish

Trim feathery fennel fronds from the fennel bulb; set aside for garnish.

Cut the fennel stalks off and discard. Peel the fennel bulb; cut it in half and remove the core. Discard the core and chop the bulb.

In a large pot, melt the butter over medium heat. Add the carrots, onions, and chopped fennel. Cook, stirring often, until the vegetables are soft but not brown, 5 to 7 minutes. Add the broth, water, gingerroot, and orange peel. Bring to a simmer, cover, and simmer for 20 minutes. Discard the orange peel.

Using an immersion blender or a blender (in batches), puree the soup until very smooth. If necessary, return the soup to the pot. If the soup is thick, add more broth to achieve desired consistency. Season with salt and pepper.

To serve, ladle soup into bowls. Top with a dollop of yogurt and garnish with reserved fennel tops.

1977

KITTY-CAT SNAPS

Living in the orphanage, Penny doesn't have many friends. But she does have one: an elderly cat named Rufus. Penny handles her friend "gingerly," even bringing him cookies as a treat! Fun to make and even more fun to eat, you'll want to share these cookies with your friends, too!

DESSERT ✦ V ✦ YIELD: About 5 dozen cookies

¾ cup butter, softened

¾ cup granulated sugar, plus more for rolling cookies

½ cup dark brown sugar

1 teaspoon baking soda

2 teaspoons ground ginger

1½ teaspoons ground cinnamon

½ teaspoon salt

½ teaspoon ground cloves

¼ teaspoon ground nutmeg

2 large eggs

⅓ cup molasses

3 tablespoons finely chopped crystallized ginger

2¼ cups all-purpose flour

Heat the oven to 375°F. Line a large rimmed baking pan with parchment paper.

In a large mixing bowl, beat the butter on medium-high for 30 seconds. Add the ¾ cup granulated sugar, brown sugar, baking soda, ground ginger, cinnamon, salt, cloves, and nutmeg. Beat until fluffy, scraping the sides of the bowl with a rubber spatula as needed, 3 to 4 minutes. Add the eggs and beat well. Beat in the molasses and crystallized ginger. Gradually beat in the flour on low, stirring in the last amount with a wooden spoon if dough gets stiff.

Place additional granulated sugar in a medium bowl. Roll the dough into 1 inch balls, then roll in the sugar.

Place the balls 2 inches apart on the prepared pan. Flatten the balls to ½ inch with the bottom of a glass or measuring cup. (You will need to bake the cookies in batches.)

Bake until cookies are cracked and done in the center, 8 to 10 minutes. Cool on the cookie sheet for 1 minute, then transfer to a wire rack to cool completely.

Repeat with remaining dough.

1977

PORCUPINE-SHAPED MEATBALLS

We could all use a friend from time to time, and Tod the fox is no different. He's not out on his own in the forest long before he encounters a porcupine who offers to share his home. These meatballs, inspired by this unlikely friendship, are perfect for sharing with your friends who need a taste of home!

ENTRÉE OR APPETIZER ✦ GF* ✦ YIELD: 6 servings

1½ pounds lean ground beef or turkey

½ cup uncooked long-grain rice

1 large egg

⅓ cup finely chopped onion

2 cloves garlic, minced

2 teaspoons dried Italian seasoning

1 teaspoon salt

½ teaspoon ground black pepper

3 tablespoons chopped fresh parsley, plus more for garnish

2 tablespoons olive oil

One 28-ounce can tomato puree

2 tablespoons tomato paste

1 tablespoon Worcestershire sauce

1 tablespoon brown sugar

In a large bowl, combine the ground beef, rice, egg, onion, garlic, Italian seasoning, salt, pepper, and chopped parsley. Using clean hands, mix the ingredients together until well combined (the mixture will be dense).

Fill a bowl with cool water. Using wet hands and working with about 3 tablespoons of the meat mixture at a time, shape the meat into oblong meatballs.

Heat the oil in a large nonstick skillet over medium-high heat. Add the meatballs and cook without moving until lightly browned, about 2 minutes. Using tongs or a metal spatula, carefully turn the meatballs over to brown other side.

In a medium bowl, stir together the tomato puree, tomato paste, Worcestershire sauce, and brown sugar. Pour the mixture over the meatballs in the skillet. Bring to a simmer. Cover and simmer on low heat until the meatballs are no longer pink in the center and the rice is tender, 25 to 30 minutes.

To serve, transfer to a serving platter and garnish with more parsley.

> **NOTE:**
> To make this dish gluten free, use a gluten-free Worcestershire sauce.

1981

NYC PUP CART CHILI DOGS

There's nothing quite like a New York City hot dog, and Dodger knows where to find the very best ones. Why should Dodger worry, when he's got Oliver in tow to help him? These chili-topped dogs are perfect for those days when you can't make it to a hot dog cart, but still want a flavor of the city!

ENTRÉE ✦ YIELD: 8 servings

FOR THE CHILI

1 tablespoon olive oil

2 slices thick-cut bacon, chopped

½ cup chopped onion

½ cup chopped green pepper

¾ pound lean ground beef

1 clove garlic, minced

One 8-ounce can tomato sauce

½ cup beef broth

1 tablespoon molasses

2 teaspoons chili powder

½ teaspoon smoked paprika

Pinch cayenne pepper (optional)

FOR THE HOT DOGS

8 all-beef kosher hot dogs

8 hot dog buns, split

FOR SERVING

Chopped red onion and shredded cheddar cheese, for topping

MAKE THE CHILI:

Heat the oil in a large skillet over medium heat. When hot, add the bacon. Cook the bacon, stirring frequently, until lightly browned and nearly crisp, 6 to 7 minutes.

Add the onion and green pepper to the skillet. Cook, stirring frequently, until onions are tender, 2 to 3 minutes. Add the ground beef and garlic. Cook, stirring frequently and breaking up the meat with a wooden spoon, until the meat is browned, about 5 minutes. Stir in the tomato sauce, broth, molasses, chili powder, paprika, and cayenne, if using. Bring to a simmer. Cook, stirring occasionally, until desired consistency, about 15 minutes. Keep warm while preparing the hot dogs.

MAKE THE HOT DOGS:

Grill the hot dogs over medium heat, or use a grill pan, until hot and nicely browned, about 7 minutes, turning at least once while grilling. Remove the hot dogs from the grill and cover with foil to keep warm. Place the split buns on the grill or grill pan. Grill until lightly toasted, 30 to 60 seconds.

Serve the grilled hot dogs in the buns, topped generously with hot chili and desired amount of onion and cheese.

1988

UNDER THE SEA CURRIED CRAB-FREE DUMPLINGS

When it comes to life on land, Sebastian knows one thing: The people up there eat fish! Ariel would never do such a thing, but that doesn't mean she can't have some tasty meals. Perhaps these crab-free dumplings would have been a better fit than the crab Chef Louis tries to serve to Ariel and Prince Eric!

ENTRÉE ✦ V, V+ ✦ YIELD: 6 servings

FOR THE DUMPLINGS

1 cup all-purpose flour

1 teaspoon baking powder

½ teaspoon salt

½ cup cold water

FOR THE CURRY

2 tablespoons vegetable oil

1 medium onion, finely chopped

½ cup chopped green pepper

1 cloves garlic, minced

2 teaspoons grated gingerroot

1 tablespoon curry powder

1 teaspoon ground turmeric

¾ teaspoon ground allspice

One 14-ounce can diced tomatoes, undrained

½ teaspoon minced Scotch bonnet or habanero chile pepper

1 teaspoon fresh thyme leaves

½ teaspoon salt

¼ teaspoon ground black pepper

Two 14-ounce cans unsweetened coconut milk

Two 7-ounce pouches unseasoned jackfruit

FOR SERVERING

Cilantro leaves

MAKE THE DUMPLINGS:

In a medium bowl, combine the all-purpose flour, baking powder, and salt. Add the water and stir with a wooden spoon to make a soft dough.

To shape the dumplings, form about 1 tablespoon of dough into a finger-size log. Flatten slightly with your fingers. Drop dumplings one at a time into a pot of boiling, salted water. Cook for 5 to 6 minutes. Remove with a slotted spoon to a lightly oiled plate. Set aside.

MAKE THE CURRY:

In a large skillet, heat the oil over medium heat. Add the onion and green pepper. Cook, stirring frequently, for 3 minutes. Add the garlic and gingerroot. Cook, stirring constantly, until fragrant, about 1 minute. Add the curry powder, turmeric, and allspice. Cook, stirring constantly, for 1 minute more.

Add the tomatoes, chile pepper, thyme, salt, and pepper. Cook and stir 3 to 4 minutes or until the tomatoes are softened. Add the coconut milk. Simmer, uncovered, for about 30 minutes or until the sauce has been reduced by one-third. Stir in the jackfruit and cooked dumplings. Heat through.

To serve, garnish with cilantro.

1989

MERMAID'S KISS

Ariel longs to be with Eric and with the world above, so much so that she has Ursula the sea witch turn her human. But to stay human, she needs to get Eric to kiss her before her three days are up. Unfortunately, that isn't as easy as it seems without her voice. But making this passion-fruit-filled drink is!

DRINK ✦ GF, V, V+ ✦ YIELD: 2 drinks

1 cup frozen passion fruit cubes, thawed

2 lime wedges (¼ of a lime)

2 tablespoons granulated sugar

Crushed ice

4 tablespoons strawberry beverage syrup

One 12-ounce can hibiscus- or guava-flavored sparkling water, chilled

2 pink hibiscus flowers, for garnish

Place the passoin fruit cubes in a small bowl. Add the lime wedges and sugar. Muddle the mixture with a wooden spoon to release the lime juice and break up the passion fruit pulp.

Fill two tall 12-ounce cocktail glasses half full of crushed ice. Pour 2 tablespoons strawberry drink syrup in each glass and divide the sparkling water between the 2 glasses.

Spoon the passion fruit mixture, including lime wedges, over the top of each glass. Garnish each glass with a hibiscus flower.

1989

CHAPTER 4

1990–1999

Under the new management of Michael Eisner and Frank G. Wells, the Disney studio brought in award-winning Broadway songwriters Alan Menken and Howard Ashman to create the music for *The Little Mermaid*. Released in 1989, *The Little Mermaid* was an instant success, winning two Academy Awards®: Best Music (Original Song) for "Under the Sea" and Best Music (Original Score). It was also the first movie to feature the experimental use of Disney's CAPS (Computer Animation Production System), a digital ink and paint system for coloring art in a computer environment. This minimized the time it took to complete a film and introduced such techniques as transparent shading and blended colors. CAPS would be used to produce every animated feature thereafter until the advent of digital technologies for completely animating with the computer.

Disney was on a roll, and it only kept getting better. In 1991, the studio released *Beauty and the Beast*. Still regarded as one of the studio's most memorable films, it was nominated for six Academy Awards®, winning Best Music (Original Song) for "Beauty and the Beast" and Best Music (Original Score). And most importantly, it was nominated for Best Picture, marking the first time an animated film had ever been nominated for that category!

The hits kept coming. In 1992, *Aladdin* was released, featuring the voice talent of the incredibly funny and endearing Robin Williams as the Genie.

The Lion King followed in 1994, featuring the all-star voices of Matthew Broderick, Nathan Lane, Jeremy Irons, and James Earl Jones and the musical talents of Sir Elton John and Sir Tim Rice. To this day, the film remains the highest-grossing traditionally animated film of all time

In 1994, Disney took to Broadway with a production of *Beauty and the Beast*, which ran for thirteen years on Broadway and toured around the world. It has been performed in more than twenty-one countries and translated into eight different languages.

The Lion King debuted on Broadway in 1997 and is still running today. It went on to win six Tony Awards®, including Best Musical, and has been translated into nine different languages and performed on every continent except Antarctica. The Walt Disney Company basked in the success of the decade, celebrating the growing representation of its films across many different forms of media, something that had never been accomplished before.

SOUP DU JOUR

Belle may not want to eat dinner with the Beast, but that's not going to stop the castle's enchanted objects from putting on a show—or from giving her an absolutely delicious dinner. And the first thing on the menu is the soup du jour: in our case, a creamy potato-leek soup that is sure to warm you on even the coldest of nights!

APPETIZER ✦ V ✦ YIELD: 6 to 8 servings

FOR THE CROUTONS

Half of a French baguette, cut into 1-inch pieces

3 tablespoons olive oil

Sea salt

FOR THE SOUP

3 large leeks, trimmed and halved lengthwise (white and light green parts)

2 tablespoons olive oil

3 small shallots, chopped

1 pound russet potatoes, peeled and coarsely chopped

6 cups low-sodium vegetable stock

1 tablespoon fresh lemon juice

½ cup heavy whipping cream

Sea salt

Freshly ground black pepper

FOR SERVING

Sour cream and chives, for garnish

MAKE THE CROUTONS:

Heat the oven to 450°F. Place the bread pieces on a large rimmed baking sheet. Drizzle with the olive oil and toss to coat. Sprinkle with a little bit of sea salt. Bake until golden brown, 5 to 6 minutes; set aside.

MAKE THE SOUP:

Rinse the leek halves under cool running water, fanning the layers to remove any sand or dirt. Pat dry and coarsely chop.

In a large pot, heat the olive oil over medium heat. Add the leeks and shallots. Cook, stirring frequently, until tender and barely browned, 6 to 8 minutes. Add the potatoes and stock. Bring to a simmer. Cover and simmer until the potatoes are very tender, 20 to 25 minutes.

Remove the pot from the heat. Use an immersion blender or blender (in batches) to blend the soup until very smooth. Return the soup to the pot, if necessary. Add the lemon juice and cream. Season to taste with salt and pepper.

Heat through and serve hot. Garnish with croutons, sour cream, and chives.

1991

HOT HORS D'OEUVRES GOUGÈRES

The enchanted objects of Beast's castle live to serve, and one of the things they serve Belle are delicious hot hors d'oeuvres. These cheese puffs are a staple at any French dinner table . . . and now they can be one at your table as well!

APPETIZER/SNACK ✦ V ✦ YIELD: About 40 cheese puffs

1 cup plus 1 tablespoon water

½ cup butter

1 teaspoon salt

1 cup all-purpose flour

Dash nutmeg

Dash ground black pepper

5 large eggs, divided

1 cup shredded Gruyère cheese

1 tablespoon water

Grated Parmesan cheese

Preheat the oven to 425°F. Line 2 large baking sheets with parchment paper.

In a large saucepan, combine 1 cup water, butter, and salt. Bring to a boil over medium-high heat. Add the flour all at once along with the nutmeg and pepper. Beat vigorously with a wooden spoon until the dough comes together and pulls away from the sides of pan. Cook and stir 1 minute more. Remove from the heat and let cool 5 minutes.

Using a wooden spoon or electric mixer, beat in 4 of the eggs, one at a time. Beat well after each addition until dough is smooth. Stir in the Gruyère cheese.

Place the dough in a large pastry bag with a 1-inch round opening. Pipe 1½-inch mounds on prepared baking sheets about 1½ inches apart. If mounds have a sharp peak, pat them down with a wet fingertip.

In a small dish, beat together the remaining egg and the water. Brush the tops of the dough mounds with the egg mixture; sprinkle with the Parmesan cheese.

Bake for 10 minutes. Reduce heat to 375°F and bake until golden brown and the cracks look dry, 20 to 25 minutes. Turn off the oven. Remove the baking sheets from the oven and pierce the puffs with a fork to allow steam to escape. Return to the warm oven and let dry for 10 minutes.

Serve hot.

TARTE AUX FRAISES WITH MRS. POTTS SPECIAL-TEA

No dinner party would be complete without a cup of tea, and Mrs. Potts is more than happy to be the one serving tea to Belle on her first night in the castle. But what if Mrs. Potts, with the help of the enchanted objects, made sure Belle had her pick of desserts, too? Perhaps, something like this delicious Tarte aux Fraises.

DESSERT & DRINK ✦ V ✦ YIELD: 8 servings

FOR THE CRUST

½ cup unsalted butter, softened, plus more for greasing the pan

⅓ cup sifted powdered sugar

1 large egg yolk

½ teaspoon salt

1¼ cups all-purpose flour

1 tablespoon half-and-half or whole milk, if needed

Butter, softened, for greasing

FOR THE CRUST:

In a food processor, combine the ½ cup butter, powdered sugar, egg yolk, salt, and flour. Pulse several times until the ingredients are combined. Pinch a bit of dough. If the mixture is too crumbly and doesn't hold together, add the half-and-half and process to combine. Gather the dough into a ball. Wrap it in plastic wrap and chill in the refrigerator for 30 minutes or until the dough can be easily rolled out.

Preheat the oven to 375°F. Grease a 9-inch tart pan with a removable bottom with softened butter.

On a lightly floured surface, roll the dough into an 11-inch circle. Carefully transfer to the prepared tart pan and press the dough into edges and up the sides of the tart pan. Patch the dough as needed to fill the tart pan and seal any cracks. Trim the dough edges to be even with the tart pan (rolling the rolling pin over the pan edge is a good way to do this). Save any extra dough.

Line the dough-filled tart pan with foil or parchment paper. Add pie weights or dried beans. Bake until the edges begin to brown, about 30 minutes. Remove the foil and pie weights. (If crust has cracked, seal it with reserved crust dough.) Return the crust to the oven and bake until golden, 5 to 10 minutes. Cool the crust completely in the pan on a wire rack.

continued on page 110

1991

continued from 109

FOR THE FILLING

12 large egg yolks, room temperature

1½ cups granulated sugar

½ cup cornstarch

2⅓ cups half-and-half

¼ cup unsalted butter

2 teaspoons vanilla bean paste or pure vanilla extract

2 tablespoons orange liqueur (optional)

2 cups sliced strawberries

Honey and lavender blossoms, for garnish

FOR MRS. POTTS SPECIAL-TEA

4 cups water

6 black tea bags

1 tablespoon culinary lavender blossoms

1 cup hot milk (about 120°F)

¼ cup honey

MAKE THE FILLING:

In a large bowl, beat the egg yolks and sugar on medium-high until thick and lemon colored, about 4 minutes. Beat in the cornstarch.

Meanwhile, in a medium saucepan, heat half-and-half over medium-high heat just until simmering. With mixer on low, gradually add the hot half-and-half to the yolk mixture. Scrape down the sides of the bowl with a rubber spatula as needed.

Pour the mixture into the saucepan. Cook, whisking constantly, over medium-low until very thick and beginning to bubble, about 4 minutes. Remove the pan from heat; stir in the butter, vanilla bean paste, and liqueur, if using. Transfer the mixture to a medium bowl. Cover the surface with plastic wrap to prevent a skin from forming. Chill in the refrigerator until cold, 2 to 4 hours.

MAKE MRS. POTTS SPECIAL-TEA:

In a teakettle or saucepan, bring the water to a boil. In a 4-cup liquid measuring cup, place 6 black tea bags and 1 tablespoon culinary lavender blossoms. Pour hot water over tea bags and blossoms. Cover and let steep for 5 minutes; strain into a large teapot. Stir in 1 cup hot milk and ¼ cup honey. Serve hot.

Carefully remove the sides of the tart pan. Spread the chilled pastry cream onto the pastry crust. Arrange the sliced strawberries on the cream. Drizzle with honey and sprinkle with lavender blossoms. Serve with Mrs. Potts Special-Tea.

ARABIAN MOON COOKIES

On his first night as a prince, Aladdin takes Jasmine on a magic carpet ride. As they soar past the moon, Jasmine revels in experiencing the freedom she's always dreamed of—thanks to Aladdin. These Arabian Moon Cookies are a reminder of that first adventure together . . . and the magical world just waiting below!

DESSERT ✦ V ✦ YIELD: About 2 dozen cookies

FOR THE DOUGH

1 cup butter, softened

1 cup granulated sugar

1 teaspoon baking powder

½ teaspoon salt

¼ teaspoon ground cardamom

3 large eggs

1 teaspoon vanilla extract

3½ cups all-purpose flour

FOR THE FILLING

1 cup dates, chopped

⅔ cup golden raisins, chopped

½ cup freshly squeezed orange juice

¼ cup honey

1 teaspoon orange zest

2 tablespoons sesame seeds

¼ cup finely chopped pistachios

Powdered sugar and silver luster dust

MAKE THE DOUGH:

In a large bowl, beat the butter on medium-high for 30 seconds. Add the sugar, baking powder, salt, and cardamom. Beat until fluffy, about 3 minutes. Beat in 2 of the eggs and vanilla until well combined. Gradually beat in the flour on low until combined, scraping down the sides of the bowl with a rubber spatula as needed. Shape the dough into a disc, wrap in plastic wrap, and chill in the refrigerator until firm, 2 to 3 hours.

MAKE THE FILLING:

In a medium saucepan, combine the dates, raisins, orange juice, and honey. Simmer over medium heat until the juice has been absorbed and the mixture is thick, about 6 minutes. Remove from the heat; stir in the orange zest, sesame seeds, and pistachios. Cool completely.

Heat the oven to 375°F. Line a cookie sheet with parchment paper.

On a lightly floured surface, roll the dough to ¼-inch thickness. Cut out the dough with 2- to 2½-inch round cookie cutters, rerolling the dough as needed. Place half of the rounds 1 inch apart on the prepared pan.

Spoon about 2 teaspoons of filling onto each of the rounds. Beat remaining egg. Brush edges with beaten egg. Place the remaining dough circles on top of filling, pressing the edges to seal. Bake until the edges are lightly browned, 8 to 10 minutes. Transfer the cookies to a wire rack to cool completely.

Dust with powdered sugar and sprinkle with silver luster dust.

1992

"NO WORRIES" MASHED POTATOES

Timon and Pumbaa like to take life easy. In fact, their motto is "Hakuna Matata." It means "no worries." They try not to think about the past—or the future. You won't have to think too far into the future either with this traditional African side dish. It's so easy to make that it takes almost no planning. So sit down, relax, and don't worry about dinner!

SIDE DISH ✦ GF, V ✦ YIELD: 4 to 6 servings

2½ pounds russet potatoes, peeled and cut into 1-inch chunks

1½ cups fresh or frozen peas

1½ cups fresh or frozen corn kernels

3 tablespoons butter

1 teaspoon salt

¼ teaspoon ground black pepper

Snipped chives or parsley

Place the potatoes in a large pot and add just enough water to cover. Bring to a boil over high heat. Reduce the heat to low, cover, and simmer for 20 minutes or until the potatoes are just tender. Add the peas and corn. Simmer for 5 minutes more. Drain, reserving about ½ cup of the cooking liquid.

Use a potato masher to mash the vegetables until the potatoes are creamy and few pieces of peas and corn remain whole. Stir in the butter until melted. Stir in a few tablespoons of the reserved cooking water to achieve the desired consistency.

Season to taste with salt and pepper. Garnish with snipped chives or parsley.

1994

PECANS WITH A VERY PLEASANT CRUNCH

If there's one thing Timon and Pumbaa can always count on finding to eat, it's a selection of tasty grubs. Slimy but satisfying, these creatures can be found all over the jungle. But it's a rare red breed that Timon likes best. While not the grubs Timon and Pumbaa eat in the film, these rare delicacies are delicious—with a very pleasant crunch.

APPETIZER/SNACK ✦ GF, V ✦ Yield: 8 to 10 servings

3 tablespoons unsalted butter

3 cups pecan halves

⅔ cup dark brown sugar

1 teaspoon salt

½ teaspoon ground cinnamon

½ teaspoon smoked paprika

⅛ teaspoon cayenne pepper

⅛ teaspoon ground black pepper

¼ cup water

1 teaspoon vanilla extract

Preheat the oven to 350°F. Line a large rimmed baking pan with parchment paper; set aside.

In a large nonstick skillet, melt the butter over medium heat. Add the pecans; cook and stir until the pecans are lightly toasted, about 3 minutes. Stir in the brown sugar. Cook and stir until the sugar is melted, about 2 minutes. Stir in the salt, cinnamon, paprika, cayenne pepper, and black pepper. Stir in the water. Bring to a simmer. Cook and stir until the water has evaporated, 1 to 2 minutes.

Remove from the heat; stir in the vanilla. Spread the nut mixture evenly on the prepared baking pan. Bake until the nuts are lightly crisp and nicely toasted, 6 to 8 minutes.

Remove from the oven and spread the nuts apart with a spoon or spatula; cool completely before serving.

1994

THREE SISTERS SUCCOTASH

Pocahontas loves her home. She was raised to respect nature, which is why her family so highly values the crops they grow—especially the corn, beans, and squash. These three foods are known as "The Three Sisters" and made up the bulk of the indigenous diet. Mixed together, they make a delicious succotash.

SIDE DISH ✦ GF, V ✦ YIELD: 6 servings

2 tablespoons butter, divided

½ cup chopped red onion or shallots

2 small zucchini, chopped

1½ cups frozen lima beans, thawed

1½ cups frozen corn kernels, thawed

¼ cup water

1 cup cherry tomatoes, halved

½ teaspoon salt

¼ teaspoon ground black pepper

3 tablespoons chopped fresh basil, plus more for garnish

1 tablespoon chopped fresh parsley, plus more for garnish

1 green onion, finely chopped (green and white parts)

In a large skillet, heat 1 tablespoon of the butter over medium heat. Add the onion; cook, stirring frequently, to soften, about 2 minutes. Add the zucchini; cook and stir 2 minutes more. Add the lima beans and corn; stir to combine. Add the water; cover and simmer for 8 to 10 minutes or until the lima beans are tender.

Add the remaining 1 tablespoon butter and stir until melted. Stir in the tomatoes, salt, and pepper. Stir in the basil, parsley, and the green onion.

Garnish with additional chopped fresh basil and parsley. Serve immediately.

1995

FEAST OF FOOLS TOPSY-TURVY CAKE

Day after day, Quasimodo watches the world from atop his bell tower, feeling sure he doesn't fit in. That is, until Topsy Turvy Day, when he dares venture out into the streets of Paris. To his surprise, Quasimodo is celebrated and crowned King of Fools. For the first time in his life, he is cheered at, not sneered at. And a delicious Feast of Fools Topsy-Turvy Cake is a perfect remedy for those days when everything is turned upside down!

DESSERT ✦ V ✦ YIELD: 12 to 16 servings

FOR THE CAKE

4¼ cups sifted cake flour, plus more for flouring the pan

¾ cup unsweetened cocoa powder

1 tablespoon baking powder

1½ teaspoons baking soda

1 teaspoon salt

2 cups unsalted butter, softened, plus more for greasing the pan

2 cups granulated sugar

1 cup light brown sugar

5 large eggs, room temperature

1 cup sour cream

1 cup whole milk

FOR THE CAKE:

Heat the oven to 350°F.

Grease with butter and flour two 6-inch round cake pans and two 8-inch round cake pans; set aside.

In a large bowl, sift together the 4¼ cups flour, cocoa powder, baking powder, baking soda, and salt.

In the bowl of a stand mixer, beat the 2 cups butter on medium-high until creamy, 30 to 60 seconds. Gradually beat in the granulated sugar and brown sugar, adding a small amount at a time, until light and fluffy, about 5 minutes. Scrape down the sides of the bowl with a rubber spatula as needed. Beat in the eggs one at a time, beating well after each addition. Beat 3 minutes more. Beat in the sour cream. Add half of the flour mixture and beat on low just until combined. Add the milk and beat just until combined. Add the remaining flour mixture. Beat on low until combined, scraping the sides of the bowl with a rubber spatula as needed. Divide the batter among the four prepared cake pans, filling each one about half full.

Bake until a toothpick inserted in the center comes out clean, 30 to 40 minutes. Cool in the pans for 5 minutes. Invert the pans to remove the cakes. Turn the cakes upright and cool completely on wire racks.

continued on page 122

1996

continued from 121

FOR THE BUTTERCREAM FROSTING

1 cup solid vegetable shortening

1 cup butter, softened

8 cups sifted powdered sugar

¼ cup whole milk

2 teaspoons vanilla extract

Dash salt

Gel paste food colorings in rose, purple, golden yellow, blue

MAKE THE BUTTERCREAM FROSTING:

In the bowl of a stand mixer, beat together the shortening and butter for 1 minute or until smooth. Gradually beat in half of the powdered sugar on low, scraping the sides of the bowl with a rubber spatula as needed. Beat in the milk, vanilla, and salt. Gradually beat in the remaining powdered sugar. (Frosting should be stiff enough to hold its shape when piped but soft enough to spread easily. Add more powdered sugar if it's too soft or beat in more milk if it's too stiff. Use at room temperature.)

To assemble the cake, use a serrated knife to level the cake tops by trimming any mounded tops. Spread a ¼-inch-thick layer of frosting over the top of one of the 6-inch cake layers. Top with remaining 6-inch layer. Repeat with the 8-inch layers. Spread a very thin layer of frosting over the sides of both layer cakes to seal in any crumbs.

To make the cake layers topsy-turvy, use the serrated knife to trim a 1-inch diagonal wedge from the tops of each of the frosted cakes, making them crooked. (Save cut pieces for another use.) Spread a thin layer of the white frosting over the cut tops to seal crumbs. Place the 6-inch cake on a 6-inch cardboard circle that is covered with foil. Place the 8-inch cake on a serving plate.

To decorate the cake, divide the remaining frosting as desired into 5 small bowls and tint them red, purple, yellow, green, and/or blue. You will need about 2 cups of one frosting color to cover the 8-inch cake and 1¼ cups of another frosting color to cover the 6-inch cake. Frost the sides and tops of both cakes.

To create support for the top cake layer, insert 4 to 6 plastic straws straight down into the 8-inch cake to the serving plate below. With scissors, trim the straws to be even with the top of the cake surface. Set the 6-inch cake (with its cardboard bottom) on top of the 8-inch cake, choosing an angle that makes the cakes look topsy-turvy. Place any remaining, colored frosting in decorating bags fitted with large round or star tips. Pipe colored frostings in stripes and dots, or as desired.

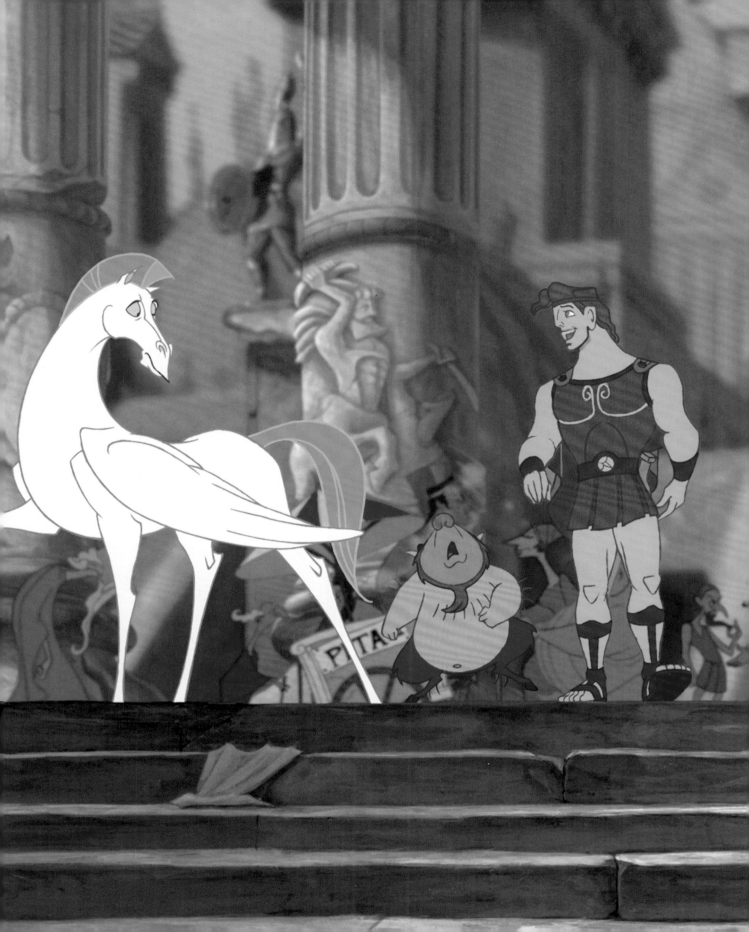

THE BIG OLIVE BREAD

When Hercules arrives in Thebes, he's wowed by the wonders of the city. As Phil tells him, if you can make it there, you can make it anywhere. Affectionately known as "The Big Olive," Thebes is a bustling city, stuffed with all sorts of people—kind of like this bread, stuffed with olives! It's a Mediterranean delight sure to leave you feeling wowed, too!

BREAD ✦ V, V+ ✦ YIELD: 12 servings

1 large whole bulb garlic

2 tablespoons olive oil

3 cups bread flour

1½ teaspoons sea salt

1 teaspoon active dry yeast

1½ cups warm water (115°F to 120°F degrees)

¾ cup coarsely chopped mixed olives

1 tablespoon finely chopped fresh rosemary

1 tablespoon finely chopped fresh oregano

Preheat the oven to 350°F.

Slice the top off the garlic bulb to expose the cloves. Place bulb on a 12-inch piece of foil. Drizzle the olive oil over top. Gather the foil around bulb and seal. Bake until soft, 30 to 40 minutes. Remove the bulb from the foil and cool completely. Squeeze the bulb to release the cloves. Coarsely chop the cloves.

In a large bowl, combine the flour, salt, and yeast. Add the warm water, garlic, olives, and herbs. Stir with a wooden spoon until all the flour is combined but still lumpy. The dough should form a loose ball shape. Cover and let rise at room temperature for 4 hours or refrigerate overnight. (If refrigerated, allow the dough to warm at room temperature for 1 hour before next step.)

Adjust the oven racks so a Dutch oven can sit on the bottom rack. Preheat the oven to 450°F.

While the oven is heating, place a heavy cast-iron or enameled cast-iron, 4- or 5-quart Dutch oven with lid in the oven.

Lightly dust a work surface with flour. Using a rubber spatula, gently roll the dough out of the bowl onto the surface without disturbing the air bubbles. With floured hands, gently scoop the edges of the dough together into a ball and place seam-side down on a 12-by-12-inch piece of parchment paper.

Remove the hot Dutch oven from the oven with hot pads. Remove the lid. Carefully transfer the parchment paper and dough to the Dutch oven. Use hot pads to replace the lid (it's okay if a little parchment paper sticks out) and place the pot back in the oven. Bake for 30 minutes.

Remove the lid and bake until the crust is golden brown and crispy, 15 to 20 minutes. Carefully remove the bread from Dutch oven. Cool on a wire rack.

1997

HAPPY-TO-SEE-YOU PORRIDGE

Breakfast on the road isn't always easy to come by, especially when you're training for battle. Luckily, Mulan has Mushu by her side, and he's ready with the most welcoming breakfast of all: congee topped with two eggs shaped like eyes, and bacon shaped like a smile. Who wouldn't want to start their day with such a friendly breakfast?

BREAKFAST ✦ YIELD: 2 servings

½ cup uncooked jasmine rice

2 cups water

2 cups chicken stock

2 green onions, finely chopped

1 teaspoon grated fresh gingerroot

Dash soy sauce

Dash sesame oil

Salt and freshly ground black pepper

2 slices bacon

4 small eggs

Place the rice in a fine-mesh strainer and rinse briefly under running water.

In a medium saucepan, bring the water and chicken stock to a boil over medium-high heat; add the rice. Reduce the heat to medium-low and simmer, stirring frequently, until the rice is tender and the porridge is the desired consistency, 20 to 30 minutes. Remove from the heat. Stir in the green onions, gingerroot, soy sauce, and sesame oil. Season to taste with salt and pepper. Keep warm.

In a large nonstick skillet, arrange the bacon in curved smile shapes and cook over medium heat until crispy, about 3 minutes per side. Transfer the bacon to a paper-towel-lined plate to drain. Do not drain bacon fat from skillet.

Return the skillet to the heat. Add the eggs and fry, without turning, until the edges are brown and crispy and the yolks are desired doneness, about 3 minutes.

Divide the porridge between 2 shallow bowls. Arrange a bacon smile and 2 fried eggs on top of each bowl of porridge.

1998

126

GINGER-PORK DUMPLINGS

Mulan was raised to put family honor above all. She knows how important it is to respect her elders, and one way she shows that respect is by sharing a meal with her family. Inspired by the dumplings Mulan's mother, Fa Li, might make, this traditional Chinese dish is perfect for any family dinner!

APPETIZER/SNACK ✦ YIELD: 48 dumplings

FOR THE SOY DIPPING SAUCE

2 tablespoons granulated sugar

¼ cup soy sauce

¼ cup water

2 tablespoons rice vinegar

1 teaspoon chile-garlic paste

½ teaspoon toasted sesame oil

½ teaspoon sesame seeds

1 teaspoon finely chopped green onion tops

FOR THE DUMPLINGS

4 tablespoons vegetable oil, divided, plus more for greasing

1 pound ground pork

2 cups classic coleslaw mix (finely chopped cabbage and carrots)

3 cloves garlic, minced

4 green onions, chopped

2 teaspoons grated fresh gingerroot

2 tablespoons hoisin sauce

1 teaspoon toasted sesame oil

½ teaspoon salt

¼ teaspoon ground black pepper

¼ teaspoon crushed red pepper

36 round pot-sticker wrappers

¼ cup water

MAKE THE SOY DIPPING SAUCE:

In a small bowl, combine the sugar, soy sauce, water, rice vinegar, chile-garlic paste, and toasted sesame oil. Whisk until the sugar is dissolved. Pour into a serving bowl. Sprinkle with the sesame seeds and finely chopped green onion tops. Set aside.

MAKE THE DUMPLINGS:

Generously grease a large baking sheet with vegetable oil.

In a large bowl, combine the pork, coleslaw mix, garlic, green onions, gingerroot, hoisin sauce, sesame oil, salt, black pepper, and crushed red pepper. Mix well to combine.

Place a few pot-sticker wrappers on a work surface. Wet the edges of the wrappers with a little water. Place about 1 tablespoon of filling in the center of each wrapper. Fold the wrappers in half; pinch and pleat the edges together to make a pouch. Place on the prepared pan, pleated side up. Repeat with remaining filling and wrappers.

Heat 2 tablespoons of oil in a large nonstick skillet over medium-high heat. Add about half of the dumplings to the skillet. Cook until the bottoms are medium-brown in color, 1 to 2 minutes.

Add the water to the skillet and immediately cover with the lid. Reduce the heat to medium-low. Steam the dumplings until most of the water has evaporated, 3 to 4 minutes. Remove the lid and cook until all the water is gone and the bottoms of the dumplings are crisp, about 1 minute. Transfer to a serving platter; cover with foil to keep warm. Repeat with remaining 2 tablespoons oil and dumplings.

Serve warm with soy dipping sauce.

1998

CHAPTER 5

2000-2009

While the 1990s had been a decade of widespread success, the 2000s saw a change in Disney's theatrical approach. Although the films released have gone on to become cult classics, many didn't have initially strong starts.

Released in 2000, *The Emperor's New Groove* featured the voice talent of comic David Spade, but didn't impress at the box office. In 2001, the film was released on home video, where it was a hit, and quickly became the top-grossing home video of the year.

Then, in 2002, Disney released *Lilo & Stitch*, a fun, hand-drawn movie about an orphan and an alien. Initially meant to take place in Kansas, filmmakers decided to shift its setting to Hawaii. It was only after a visit to Kauai that the filmmakers realized how strongly Hawaiians carry the spirit of 'Ohana with them and decided to incorporate it into the film.

Lilo & Stitch was a critical success, hailed by Roger Ebert as "one of the most charming feature-length cartoons of recent years—funny, sassy, startling, original." *Lilo & Stitch* ranked number two at the box office on its opening weekend and would go on to sell more than 3 million DVDs the day it was released for home viewing. The movie was such a success that it inspired three movie sequels and three television shows.

Throughout the 2000s, the studio released a host of other films destined to become fan favorites, including *Brother Bear* (2003), *Chicken Little* (2005), and *Bolt* (2008). But change had come. In 2005, Bob Iger was named CEO of the Walt Disney Company. This brought about a creative transition as to what films were developed and how they were produced.

In 2007, the Company's feature animation studio was renamed Walt Disney Animation Studios, and a decision was made to return to Disney's roots. The result was the first fairy tale reimagining in 16 years: 2009's *The Princess and the Frog*, which has grown to be a beloved film.

ROASTED PURPLE PERUVIAN POTATOES

As his village's leader, Pacha knows how important it is to care for his villagers. He knows that life as a farmer is hard, but also rewarding. That's why Pacha puts so much effort into working his land. This delicious potato dish, inspired by those that Pacha may have grown on his farm, is sure to be a staple at any Incan farmer's table!

SIDE DISH ✦ GF, V, V+ ✦ YIELD: 6 servings

2 pounds purple potatoes, cut into 1½-inch pieces (see note)

3 tablespoons olive oil

1 teaspoon salt

1 teaspoon aji amarillo chile powder (or hot paprika) (see note)

1 teaspoon smoked paprika

½ teaspoon ground cumin

½ teaspoon garlic powder

½ teaspoon dried oregano

¼ teaspoon ground black pepper

Chopped fresh parsley

Heat the oven to 375°F.

On a large rimmed baking pan, toss the potatoes with the olive oil to coat. In a small bowl, combine the salt, chile powder, paprika, cumin, garlic powder, oregano, and pepper. Sprinkle over the potatoes and toss to coat.

Spread the potatoes into a single layer. Roast for 20 minutes. Turn and roast until golden brown and tender, about 15 minutes more.

Sprinkle with the parsley.

Aji amarillo is a Peruvian yellow chile pepper that packs a fair amount of heat.

NOTE:
It's most common to find tiny new purple potatoes, which do not need to be peeled. If you are able to find regular-size purple potatoes, peel for more purple color.

2000

MUDKA'S MEAT HUT MUG OF MEAT

Kuzco and Pacha are on the run, and there aren't many places to hide. Luckily, they manage to find temporary sanctuary at Mudka's Meat Hut, a local diner known for its specialty: the Mug of Meat! This amazing dish, inspired by the one invented by the diner's owner, Major Mudka, more than fifty years ago, is sure to leave you more than satisfied!

ENTRÉE ✦ GF ✦ YIELD: 1 serving

Vegetable oil, for greasing

4 ounces extra-lean ground beef

1 large egg, beaten

2 tablespoons uncooked instant rice

2 tablespoons ketchup, plus more for garnish

1 tablespoon chopped black olives, plus more for garnish

1 tablespoon chopped canned green chiles

1 tablespoon frozen corn kernels, plus more for garnish

½ teaspoon smoked paprika

½ teaspoon chile powder

⅛ teaspoon ground cumin

Pinch onion powder

Pinch salt and pepper

Grease a large (10- to 12-ounce) microwave-safe mug with vegetable oil.

In a medium bowl, combine the beef, egg, rice, ketchup, olives, chiles, corn, paprika, chile powder, cumin, onion powder, and salt and pepper to taste. Mix well with a fork or your hands. Shape into a ball.

Place the meat ball into the mug. Press the meat ball down slightly to fill the mug evenly. Cover with vented plastic wrap.

Microwave on high for 3 minutes or until no longer pink in center and an instant-read thermometer inserted into the center registers 165°F. Cool 5 minutes before serving.

Warm about 1 tablespoon of corn kernels in a microwave-safe cup in the microwave for 5 seconds. Garnish the meatloaf with a squiggle of ketchup, olives, and warmed corn kernels.

ROAD-TO-ATLANTIS TURKEY JERKY

For any extended expedition, it's always a good idea to bring along a talented chef. Unfortunately for the crew seeking out the lost city of Atlantis, they have Jebidiah Allardyce "Cookie" Farnsworth—the worst chef around. Milo could pack plenty of Turkey Jerky like this to keep himself full and ready to explore!

APPETIZER/SNACK ✦ GF* ✦ YIELD: 8 servings

2 pounds skinless, boneless turkey breast

½ cup 100% pineapple juice

¼ cup reduced-sodium soy sauce

1 tablespoon Worcestershire sauce

1 tablespoon honey

2 teaspoons smoked paprika

1 teaspoon garlic powder

1 teaspoon ground black pepper

1 teaspoon sriracha, sauce (optional)

Olive oil cooking spray

Halve the turkey breast horizontally. Place on a large rimmed sheet pan in a single layer. Freeze the turkey pieces until partially frozen, about 20 minutes (this makes it easier to slice thinly in the next step).

Slice the turkey into thin slices, ⅛- to ¼-inch thickness. Place in a large bowl. Add the pineapple juice, soy sauce, Worcestershire sauce, honey, paprika, garlic powder, black pepper, and sriracha, if using. Mix well. Cover and marinate in refrigerator for at least 4, or up to 24, hours.

Place the turkey in a colander and drain well. Heat the oven to 200°F.

Line a large rimmed baking pan with foil. Place a wire rack on the pan. Spray the rack with cooking spray. Arrange the turkey pieces in a single layer on the rack. Bake for 2 hours. Turn the turkey pieces over and bake until dry and chewy, about 2 hours more. Let cool completely.

Store in an airtight container in the refrigerator for up to 2 weeks.

> **NOTE:**
> To make this recipe gluten free, use a gluten-free Worcestershire sauce.

2001

LŪʻAU BLUE HAWAIIAN DRINK

Lilo spends a lot of time at the lūʻau where Nani works. Although she often wishes she could be somewhere else, she does enjoy getting the lūʻau's tasty non-alcoholic drinks—especially when they come with an umbrella!

DRINK ✦ GF, V, V+ ✦ YIELD: 4 servings

FOR THE GINGER-LIME SYRUP

½ cup raw (demerara) sugar

½ cup water

3 slices fresh gingerroot

1 teaspoon lime zest

FOR THE DRINK

8 ounces 100% pineapple juice, chilled

8 ounces coconut water chilled

Two 12-ounce cans unsweetened lemon- or lime-flavored sparkling water, chilled

Several teaspoons butterfly pea flower extract

Ice cubes

FOR SERVING

Pineapple wedges, paper umbrellas, edible mini orchid flowers, for garnish

MAKE THE GINGER-LIME SYRUP:

In a small saucepan, combine the sugar, water, gingerroot, and lime zest. Bring to a boil over medium-high heat. Remove from the heat; cover and let steep for 10 minutes. Remove the ginger slices.

MAKE THE DRINK:

In a pitcher, combine the ginger-lime syrup, pineapple juice, coconut water, and sparkling water. Add enough pea flower extract to make desired color.

Serve in tall cocktail glasses over ice. Garnish with pineapple wedges, paper umbrellas, and orchid flowers.

2002

POLYNESIAN SWEET POTATOES

As Lilo's caretaker, Nani knows it's her job to take care of Lilo. And that means making sure she eats well! Luckily, you can eat well, too, with this creamy sweet potato mash infused with the freshest Hawaiian coconut milk!

SIDE DISH ✦ GF, V ✦ YIELD: 6 servings

2 pounds sweet potatoes, peeled and cut into 2-inch chunks

6 tablespoons unsalted butter, cut into chunks, divided, plus more for greasing the dish

1 teaspoon salt

½ teaspoon ground ginger

½ teaspoon ground turmeric

¼ teaspoon ground coriander

½ teaspoon ground cinnamon, divided

⅓ cup canned full-fat coconut milk (shake can before measuring)

½ cup chopped macadamia nuts

3 tablespoons brown sugar

Heat the oven to 350°F.

Place the sweet potatoes into a large saucepan and add enough water to cover. Bring to a boil over high heat; reduce heat to low and cover. Simmer until the potatoes are very tender, 35 to 40 minutes. Drain well; return the potatoes to the saucepan.

Mash the potatoes with a potato masher or beat with an electric mixer. Stir in 4 tablespoons of the butter, salt, ginger, turmeric, coriander, and ¼ teaspoon of the cinnamon. Stir in the coconut milk. Spread the mixture in a 1½-quart casserole dish greased with butter.

In a medium skillet, melt the remaining 2 tablespoons butter over medium heat. Add the nuts and brown sugar and cook, stirring constantly, until the sugar is dissolved and nuts are lightly toasted. Stir in the remaining ¼ teaspoon cinnamon. Spoon over the potatoes in the casserole dish.

Bake until heated through, 25 to 30 minutes.

2002

ALPONIAN CHOWDER WITH EXTRA SOLARIS SEED

At the Benbow Inn, there's always something tasty on the menu. But of all the delicious options on the menu, it's the Alponian chowder that Dr. Delbert Doppler likes best—with extra Solaris seed, of course!

ENTRÉE ✦ YIELD: 8 servings

1 tablespoon olive oil

One 12-ounce package smoked kielbasa sausage, cut into 1-inch chunks

½ cup chopped onion

½ cup chopped green pepper

3 cups chicken broth

1 large russet potato, peeled and cut in 1-inch pieces

1 cup coarsely chopped green cabbage

1 teaspoon fennel seed, crushed, plus more for serving

½ teaspoon salt

¼ teaspoon ground black pepper

1½ cups half-and-half or whole milk

3 tablespoons all-purpose flour

½ cup frozen corn kernels

2 slices bacon, cooked crisp and crumbled

Chopped fresh parsley, for garnish

In a large pot, heat the oil over medium-high heat until shimmering. Add the sausage and cook, stirring occasionally, until browned, 2 to 3 minutes. Add the onion and green pepper. Cook, stirring frequently, until the onion is softened, 3 to 4 minutes. Add the chicken broth, potato, cabbage, fennel seed, salt, and pepper. Bring to a boil; reduce heat to medium-low. Cover and simmer 10 to 15 minutes or until the potatoes are tender.

In a measuring cup, whisk together the half-and-half and flour. Add to the pot. Turn heat to medium. Cook and stir until slightly thickened and bubbly, 4 to 5 minutes. Stir in the corn.

Ladle into soup bowls and top with the bacon, parsley, and additional fennel seed.

2002

BONZABEAST STEW

There's not always much time onboard a pirate ship to make a tasty meal. Luckily, John Silver is quick with his hands—or rather, his cybernetic tools. He wastes no time whipping up a Bonzabeast Stew for his hungry crew. This hearty meal is filling enough to satisfy a whole ship full of pirates!

ENTRÉE ✦ YIELD: 6 to 8 servings

¼ cup all-purpose flour

¼ cup canola oil

1 cup chopped celery

1 cup chopped onion

1 cup chopped green pepper

3 cloves garlic, minced

4 cups chicken broth

2 teaspoons seafood seasoning

¼ teaspoon ground black pepper

⅛ teaspoon cayenne pepper

1½ pounds large shrimp, peeled and deveined

One 14-ounce can diced tomatoes

½ cup frozen peas

Hot cooked rice

Chopped parsley, for garnish

In a large pot, whisk together the flour and oil. Cook, whisking constantly, over medium heat until golden brown, about 10 minutes, being careful not to burn (reduce heat if needed).

Stir in the celery, onion, and green pepper. Cook, stirring frequently, until the vegetables are tender, 5 to 6 minutes. Add the garlic and cook, stirring constantly, for 1 minute.

Add the broth, seafood seasoning, black pepper, and cayenne. Stir to combine. Increase the heat to medium-high and bring to a boil. Add the shrimp and tomatoes. Simmer for 3 to 4 minutes or until the shrimp is opaque. Stir in the peas.

Ladle the stew into soup bowls. Top with a scoop of rice and some parsley.

2002

NUT-CRUSTED SALMON WITH CRANBERRY RELISH

When Kenai is turned into a bear, his whole life is turned upside down. Determined to become human again, he sets off on a quest to find his family. But all that journeying is hard work. Luckily, there's nothing bears like more than some fresh salmon, and the river is full of it. This tasty salmon dish, paired with the cranberries and hazelnuts that grow wild in Alaska, is sure to please any hungry bear—or human!

ENTRÉE ✦ GF* ✦ YIELD: 4 servings

FOR THE SAUCE

2 cups fresh or frozen cranberries

1 cup fresh or frozen blueberries

½ cup granulated sugar

2 teaspoons orange zest

¼ teaspoon ground cinnamon

¼ teaspoon ground black pepper

¼ cup water

FOR THE SALMON

Four 6- to 8-ounce salmon fillets, ¾-inch thick

1 large egg, lightly beaten

¼ cup whole milk

2 teaspoons Dijon mustard

⅔ cup panko breadcrumbs

⅔ cup finely chopped hazelnuts

½ teaspoon salt

¼ teaspoon ground black pepper

2 tablespoons canola oil

NOTE:
To make this dish gluten free, use gluten-free panko breadcrumbs.

MAKE THE SAUCE:

In a medium saucepan, combine the cranberries, blueberries, sugar, orange zest, cinnamon, pepper, and water. Bring to a boil over medium-high. Reduce heat to medium-low and simmer, uncovered, until the cranberries pop, about 10 minutes. Remove the pan from the heat and cool to room temperature.

MAKE THE SALMON:

Pat the salmon dry with paper towels.

In a shallow dish, beat together the egg, milk, and mustard. In another shallow dish, stir together the breadcrumbs, hazelnuts, salt, and pepper.

In a large nonstick skillet, heat the oil over medium-high heat. Dip the fish fillets into the egg mixture, then into the nut mixture. Place in the hot skillet. Cook until browned on the bottoms, 2 to 3 minutes. Turn and cook until the fish flakes easily with a fork, 2 to 3 minutes more.

Serve the fish fillets with the sauce.

2003

LITTLE PATCH OF HEAVEN CUSTARD PIE

As a dairy farmer, Pearl has her fair share of milk and cream. And like any farmer, she knows how to make the most of them. This flaky pie filled with custard, inspired by life on Pearl's farm, is like its own patch of heaven.

DESSERT ✦ V ✦ YIELD: 8 servings

FOR THE CRUST

1¼ cups all-purpose flour

2 teaspoons granulated sugar

½ teaspoon salt

½ cup cold unsalted butter, cut up

¼ to ⅓ cup cold water

1 teaspoon cider vinegar

MAKE THE CRUST:

In a medium bowl, combine the flour, sugar, and salt. Cut in the butter with a pastry blender or 2 knives until the butter is the size of small peas.

In a small bowl, stir together the cold water and vinegar. Sprinkle about half of the water mixture over flour the mixture. Toss with a fork to combine. Add enough of the remaining water mixture to moisten all of the flour mixture until the dough can be shaped into a ball. Flatten the dough into a disc. Wrap in plastic wrap and chill in the refrigerator for 30 minutes.

Heat the oven to 450°F.

On a lightly floured surface, roll out the dough to a 12-inch circle. Transfer to a 9-inch pie plate. Trim the edge of dough ½ inch beyond the pie plate. Turn the dough edge under. Pinch and pleat the crust edge as desired.

Line the pie crust with a double layer of foil. Fill with pie weights (or dry beans). Bake for 8 minutes.

Remove the foil and pie weights and bake for 6 to 8 minutes more or until golden brown. Set aside. Reduce the oven temperature to 325°F.

continued on page 149

2004

continued from 146

FOR THE FILLING

1¼ cups whole milk

1 cup heavy whipping cream

4 large eggs

½ cup granulated sugar

¼ teaspoon salt

2 teaspoons vanilla extract

Freshly grated nutmeg

MAKE THE FILLING:

In a medium saucepan, combine the milk and cream. Heat over medium heat just until hot enough to get bubbles around the edges, but not to a simmer. Remove from the heat.

In a medium bowl, whisk together the eggs, sugar, and salt. Gradually whisk one-quarter of the milk mixture into the egg mixture. Pour the egg mixture into the saucepan with the remaining milk mixture, whisking constantly to combine. Pour the filling through a mesh strainer set over a large bowl to remove any pieces of cooked egg; stir the vanilla into the custard in the bowl. Discard any bits of cooked eggs left in the strainer.

Place the baked crust on the middle oven rack. Pour the filling into the crust. Sprinkle the top with nutmeg. Cover the pie crust edge with foil to prevent overbrowning.

Bake for 25 minutes. Remove the foil. Bake until the custard is set around the edges and a knife inserted in the center comes out clean, 10 to 15 minutes more.

Cool on a wire rack for 1 hour. Chill the pie within 2 hours of baking. The pie can be served warm or chilled.

COMMANDER LITTLE HERO SANDWICH

After a long day of saving Oakey Oaks from being taken over by aliens, Commander Little needs to refuel. And a perfect way for a hero to re-energize is with a tasty hero sandwich, a favorite hearty meal for a hero like Commander Little!

ENTRÉE ✦ V ✦ YIELD: 4 servings

¼ cup mayonnaise

1 tablespoon coarse-ground brown mustard

¼ teaspoon cracked black pepper

Two 8-inch sub rolls, split

2 tablespoons olive oil

2 large portobello mushrooms, stemmed, gills removed (see note)

1 large red bell pepper, stemmed, seeded, and halved

Half of a medium red onion, cut in ½-inch-thick slices

Salt and ground black pepper

4 ounces sliced provolone cheese

Dill or sweet pickle slices

Pickled sweet cherry peppers or pepperoncini peppers

In a small bowl, stir together the mayonnaise, mustard, and cracked pepper; set aside.

Heat a grill pan over medium-high heat. Brush the cut sides of the rolls lightly with some of the olive oil. Place cut side down on the grill pan. Grill until lightly toasted, 30 to 60 seconds. Spread the toasted buns with mustard spread. Set aside.

Place the mushrooms, pepper halves, and red onion in a large bowl. Drizzle with the remaining oil. Season with salt and pepper to taste. Toss to combine.

Working in batches, grill the vegetables on both sides until tender and well browned from the pan, about 4 minutes per side. Slice the grilled mushrooms and pepper halves. Separate the onion into rings. Arrange the grilled vegetables on the toasted buns. Top with cheese slices, pickle slices, and pickled peppers.

Add the bun tops; cut the sandwiches in half and serve immediately.

> **NOTE:**
> To remove the gills from portobello mushrooms, scrape with a spoon.

2005

MEATBALL CANNON MEATBALLS IN GRAVY

Family dinner is a bit different in the Robinson household, where meatballs are launched by cannons, food fights are commonplace, and gravy is delivered on a gravy train . . . literally! This small train runs around the table delivering gravy to anyone who needs it for their meatballs. A perfect addition to a standard meatball dinner—just watch out reaching for the gravy. You may get hit by a meatball!

ENTRÉE ✦ YIELD: 4 servings

FOR THE MEATBALLS

¼ cup dry breadcrumbs

¼ cup whole milk

8 ounces lean ground pork

8 ounces lean ground beef

2 tablespoons finely chopped yellow onion

½ teaspoon salt

¼ teaspoon ground black pepper

Pinch ground nutmeg

2 tablespoons canola oil

MAKE THE MEATBALLS:

In a medium bowl, combine the breadcrumbs and milk. Let stand for 5 minutes to soften.

Add the pork, beef, onion, salt, pepper, and nutmeg. Mix until well combined using hands or a wooden spoon. For each meatball, scoop about 1 tablespoon of meat mixture and shape into a ball. (To keep the meat mixture from sticking, dip your hands in cool water every so often.)

In a large skillet, heat the oil over medium-high heat. Add the meatballs to the skillet and cook until golden brown on all sides, turning occasionally, about 10 minutes. Transfer the meatballs to a plate.

continued on page 154

2007

continued from 153

FOR THE MASHED POTATOES

3 medium russet potatoes, peeled and cut into chunks

½ cup whole milk

2 tablespoons butter

⅓ cup sour cream

½ teaspoon salt, plus more for cooking water

¼ teaspoon ground black pepper

FOR THE GRAVY

1 cup hot water (about 140°F)

⅔ cup half-and-half

3 tablespoons all-purpose flour

¼ teaspoon salt

¼ teaspoon ground black pepper

½ teaspoon soy sauce

FOR SERVING

Chopped fresh parsley, for garnish

MAKE THE MASHED POTATOES:

Place the potatoes in a large saucepan. Add water to cover; salt the water generously.

Bring to a boil over high heat. Reduce heat to medium and cook until potatoes are tender when pierced with a fork, about 20 minutes.

Drain potatoes and return to the pan. Add the milk, butter, sour cream, salt, and black pepper. Mash over low heat with a potato masher until desired consistency, adding more milk, if necessary. Remove from heat. Cover and keep warm while you make the gravy.

MAKE THE GRAVY:

Add the hot water to the skillet used for the meatballs over medium heat. Scrape the bottom of the skillet with a wooden spoon to loosen any browned bits. Bring to a simmer.

In a measuring cup, whisk together the half-and-half and flour. Add all at once to the skillet. Cook, stirring constantly, until thickened and bubbly, 3 to 4 minutes. Stir in the salt, pepper, and soy sauce.

Return the meatballs to the skillet. Turn the meatballs over in the gravy and cook until heated through, about 5 minutes.

Sprinkle with parsley and serve with the mashed potatoes.

WAFFLE WORLD CHICKEN AND WAFFLES

When Bolt asks Mittens for help finding Penny, the feisty cat shows him a "top-top-secret map of the entire world." That is, a map showing all the Waffle World locations across the country. Finding every Waffle World may not be the answer to finding Penny, but a bite of chicken and waffles is enough to fuel you up for any search!

ENTRÉE (BREAKFAST) ✦ YIELD: 4 to 6 servings

FOR THE CHICKEN

1 cup buttermilk

1 large egg

1 tablespoon hot sauce

1 cup all-purpose flour

½ teaspoon garlic powder

½ teaspoon salt

½ teaspoon ground black pepper

Canola oil or peanut oil, for frying

1½ pounds chicken tenders

MAKE THE CHICKEN:

Heat the oven to 300°F. Place a wire rack on a large rimmed baking pan; set aside.

In a shallow dish, whisk together the buttermilk, egg, and hot sauce. In another shallow dish, combine the flour, garlic powder, salt, and pepper.

In a large pot, heat 2 inches of the oil over medium heat to 350°F.

Roll a few pieces of chicken in the flour mixture. Dip in the buttermilk mixture, then roll again in the flour mixture. Carefully add to the hot oil. Fry until golden brown and the chicken is cooked through, 6 to 7 minutes, turning as needed. Remove with a slotted spoon or tongs. Place on the prepared baking pan. Keep warm in the oven while frying the rest of the chicken and making the waffles.

continued on page 158

2008

continued from 157

FOR THE WAFFLES

1¾ cups all-purpose flour

2 tablespoons granulated sugar

2 teaspoons baking powder

½ teaspoon baking soda

¼ teaspoon salt

2 large eggs, yolks and whites separated

2 cups buttermilk

1 jalapeño, finely chopped (seeded if desired)

½ cup butter, melted and cooled

Nonstick cooking spray

FOR SERVING

1 cup pure maple syrup, warmed

MAKE THE WAFFLES:

Heat a waffle maker. In a medium bowl, whisk together the flour, sugar, baking powder, baking soda, and salt. In another medium bowl, beat the 2 egg whites with an electric mixer until stiff peaks form, 5 to 6 minutes; set aside.

In a large bowl, whisk together the buttermilk, egg yolks, jalapeño, and melted butter. Stir in the flour mixture just until combined. (Do not overmix or waffles will be tough.) Fold in the egg whites. (Batter will be slightly lumpy.)

Spray the waffle maker with nonstick cooking spray. Add the batter according to the waffle maker manufacturer's instructions and cook the waffles until brown and crispy. Repeat with remaining batter, spraying the waffle maker with nonstick spray as needed.

To serve, place waffle squares on plates. Top with chicken fingers and drizzle with syrup.

BEST GUMBO YOU'VE EVER TASTED

Even as a little girl, Tiana knew one day she wanted to become a chef. And she's got the best teacher in the world: her father, James. But Tiana's skills surpass even that of her father, which she proves when she makes a pot of gumbo that James declares, "the best gumbo I've ever tasted." This deliciously Cajun dish is perfect for sharing with family, friends, or the whole neighborhood!

ENTRÉE ✦ YIELD: 8 servings

½ cup canola oil

½ cup all-purpose flour

1 medium onion, chopped

1 medium green pepper, chopped

2 stalks celery, chopped

2 cloves garlic, minced

1 teaspoon fresh thyme leaves or ½ teaspoon dried thyme

2 teaspoons Creole seasoning

2 teaspoons smoked paprika

½ teaspoon ground black pepper

⅛ teaspoon cayenne pepper

1 bay leaf

One 14.5-ounce can fire-roasted tomatoes

4 cups chicken broth

3 tablespoons butter

8 ounces smoked andouille sausage, sliced

8 ounces spicy dry-cured sausage, chopped

1 cup fresh okra, sliced

1½ pounds large shrimp, peeled and deveined

1 teaspoon gumbo filé powder (optional)

Sliced green onion, for garnish

In a large pot, whisk together the oil and flour. Heat over medium heat, whisking constantly, until it turns a deep brown color, about 20 minutes. Do not burn.

Add the onion, green pepper, and celery. Cook, stirring frequently, until the vegetables are very tender, about 10 minutes. Add the garlic. Cook, stirring constantly, 2 minutes more. Add the thyme, Creole seasoning, paprika, black pepper, cayenne, and the bay leaf. Cook, stirring constantly, for 1 minute. Add the tomatoes and broth. Cook, stirring frequently, until broth comes to a simmer. Cover and simmer over low heat for 20 minutes.

In a large skillet, heat the butter over medium-high heat. Add the andouille sausage, spicy sausage, and okra. Cook, stirring frequently, until lightly browned, about 8 minutes. Stir the sausage mixture into the broth mixture.

Add the shrimp and cook until the shrimp is opaque, 3 to 4 minutes. Stir in the filé powder, if using. Remove the bay leaf.

Ladle into soup bowls. Top with green onion slices.

2009

LOUIS MUFFULETTAS

New Orleans is known for its food, and poor Louis is dying to taste some of it. But an alligator going into a restaurant isn't likely to end well, which means that Louis will have to keep dreaming of these delicious muffuletta po'boys . . . at least for now!

ENTRÉE ✦ YIELD: 8 to 10 servings

FOR THE FOCACCIA

4½ to 5 cups bread flour or all-purpose flour, divided

1 teaspoon salt

1 tablespoon dried Italian seasoning, divided

One 0.25-ounce package active dry yeast

4 tablespoons olive oil, divided, plus more for greasing the bowl

1¼ cups lukewarm water (110°F to 115°F)

2 tablespoons grated Parmesan cheese

¾ teaspoon flaky sea salt

MAKE THE FOCACCIA:

In a large bowl, combine 3 cups of the flour, the salt, 1 teaspoon of the Italian seasoning, and yeast. Add 2 tablespoons of the olive oil and the water; mix with a wooden spoon until combined. Stir in enough of the remaining flour to make a soft dough that is still a bit sticky. Shape the dough into a ball. Place the dough into an oiled bowl, turning once to coat the dough. Cover and let rise in a warm place until doubled in size, 60 to 90 minutes.

Line a large rimmed baking sheet with parchment paper. Lightly oil the parchment paper. Roll the dough out onto the oiled parchment. Divide the dough in half. Gently pat each portion into a long rectangle (about 4-by-12-inches each). Sprinkle the top of the dough with the remaining 2 teaspoons Italian seasoning, Parmesan cheese, and flaky sea salt. Cover loosely and let rise until puffy, 30 to 45 minutes.

Place a baking stone in the oven and heat to 425°F. When the dough is ready, use your fingers to gently dimple the dough all over. Slide the dough and parchment paper onto the heated baking stone (or place the dough, parchment paper, and baking pan directly into oven).

Bake until lightly browned, 20 to 25 minutes. While warm, brush the loaves with the remaining 2 tablespoons olive oil. Place loaves on a rack to cool.

2009

FOR THE SANDWICHES

One 16-ounce jar giardiniera (Italian pickled vegetables), drained and roughly chopped

1 cup green olives with pimiento, roughly chopped

⅔ cup sliced pepperoncini peppers

½ cup chopped carrots

½ cup chopped celery

3 cloves garlic, minced

2 tablespoons capers, chopped

1 teaspoon anchovy paste (optional)

½ cup Italian salad dressing

1 pound sliced deli ham

1 pound sliced deli salami

8 ounces deli sliced provolone cheese

8 ounces deli sliced Swiss cheese

Salt and ground black pepper

MAKE THE SANDWICHES:

Using a serrated knife, split each loaf in half horizontally.

In a medium bowl, combine the giardiniera, olives, pepperoncini, carrots, celery, garlic, capers, and anchovy paste, if using. Stir in the Italian dressing.

Layer the ham, salami, provolone cheese, and Swiss cheese on top of the focaccia bottoms. Spoon the vegetable mixture on top. Season to taste with salt and plenty of ground black pepper.

Place the focaccia tops and press down with your hands to compress the sandwiches a bit. Cut each sandwich loaf into serving-size pieces. Whole loaves can be wrapped tightly in plastic wrap and stored in the refrigerator for up to 2 hours.

BIG DADDY BEIGNETS

Tiana may make the best gumbo around, but it's her beignets that really make her stand out. A staple of New Orleans life, Tiana's beignets are made with lots of heart . . . which may be why Charlotte wants her father to buy so many of them for her party. She's hoping one taste will land her the heart of a prince!

BREAD ✦ V ✦ YIELD: 36 beignets

2¾ to 3¼ cups all-purpose flour, divided

One 0.25-ounce package active dry yeast

¼ teaspoon ground nutmeg

1 cup whole milk

¼ cup granulated sugar

2 tablespoons shortening or butter

½ teaspoon salt

1 large egg

Vegetable oil for deep frying, plus more for greasing the bowl

Powdered sugar

Honey

In a large mixing bowl, combine 1¼ cups of the flour, the yeast, and nutmeg.

In a small saucepan, combine the milk, sugar, shortening, and salt. Heat and stir over medium-low until warm (120°F to 130°F) and the shortening is nearly melted. Add the warm milk mixture and egg to the flour mixture. Beat with an electric mixer on low for 30 seconds to combine, then beat for 3 minutes on high. Stir in enough of the remaining flour with a wooden spoon to make a soft dough.

On a lightly floured surface, shape the dough into a ball. Place the dough in a greased bowl, turning once to coat the surface of the dough. Cover and chill the dough in the refrigerator for at least 4 hours or overnight.

On a lightly floured surface, roll the dough to an 18-by-12-inch rectangle. Cut the dough into thirty-six 3-by-2-inch rectangles. Cover and let rest for 30 minutes.

In a large saucepan or deep fryer, heat 2 inches of oil to 375°F. Place a wire rack on a large baking pan and cover with paper towels. Fry 2 to 3 dough rectangles at a time for about 1 minute, turning once. Remove with a slotted spoon and drain on the paper towels. Return the oil to 375°F and repeat with the remaining dough.

Serve warm, dusted generously with powdered sugar and drizzled with honey.

2009

CHAPTER 6

2010–PRESENT

Although Walt Disney Animation Studios had seen a string of successes in the early 2010s including *Tangled* (2010) and *Wreck-It Ralph* (2012), no one was prepared for the incredible success that was *Frozen* (2013). The movie was nominated for ten Academy Awards® and went on to win four, including the Academy Award® for Best Animated Feature—a category started in 2001 that had been awarded to multiple Pixar movies, but never to a Disney Animation film until that year!

Walt Disney Animation Studios would follow that success with other critically successful and popular films including the Academy Award®-winning *Big Hero 6* (2014), Academy Award®-winning *Zootopia* (2016), *Moana* (2016), and *Frozen 2* (2019).

The 2020s saw several feature films being nearly simultaneously released in theaters and on streaming platforms, an example being *Raya and the Last Dragon* (2021). Among the decade's highs is the charming film *Encanto* (2022). The story about a young woman trying to find her own magic found extreme success on the streaming service Disney+ and spawned the catchphrase and song "We Don't Talk About Bruno," which quickly became commonly used in households across the world. Unlike most feature films, which have only two or three main characters, *Encanto* features a dozen main characters—a unique challenge for the animation team to pull off. Music by superstar Lin-Manuel Miranda, who had also written music for *Moana* (2016), helped launch *Encanto* to be Disney's most successful movie of the 2020s . . . so far!

The 2020s promise to continue to be an exciting decade for Disney. From 2022's *Strange World*, which received critical praise, to 2023's *Wish*, the story of a sharp-witted idealist who makes a powerful wish on a star, it's no wonder that Disney has been an integral part of our lives for more than a century!

PARMESAN-GARLIC BRAIDED SKILLET BREAD

Rapunzel never leaves home without her trusty skillet! When not being used to knock intruders unconscious, it can be used to cook up some delicious meals. Inspired by Rapunzel's signature braid, this crisscrossed bread is sure to become your signature, too—signature recipe, that is!

BREAD ✦ V ✦ YIELD: 24 (1-slice) servings

FOR THE DOUGH

1 large russet potato, peeled and cubed

2 cups water

¼ cup butter, softened

½ teaspoon salt

½ teaspoon ground turmeric

¼ teaspoon saffron threads

4½ to 4¾ cups all-purpose flour, divided

Two 0.25-ounce packages active dry yeast

2 large eggs

Olive oil, for greasing

MAKE THE DOUGH:

In a medium saucepan, combine the potato and water. Bring to a boil over high heat. Reduce heat to medium-low and simmer until the potato is very tender, 12 to 15 minutes. Drain, reserving 1 cup of the hot cooking liquid in a glass measuring cup. Add the butter, salt, turmeric, and saffron to the reserved cooking liquid. Cool to 120°F to 130°F. Mash the cooked potato in the pan and set aside.

In a large bowl, whisk together 2 cups of the flour and the yeast. Add the warm saffron mixture and the eggs. Beat with an electric mixer on low for 30 seconds to combine. Beat on high speed for 3 minutes. With a wooden spoon, stir in the mashed potato and enough of the remaining flour to make a soft dough.

On a lightly floured surface, knead in enough of the remaining flour to make a moderately stiff, smooth, and elastic dough, about 5 minutes. Generously grease a large bowl with olive oil. Shape the dough into a ball and place in the bowl. Turn dough to oil the surface; cover and let rise in a warm place until doubled in size, 60 to 90 minutes.

Generously grease a 10- to 12-inch, cast-iron skillet with olive oil; set aside.

Punch down the dough; place on a lightly floured surface. Let rest for 10 minutes. Roll the dough out to a 20-by-12-inch rectangle.

continued on page 170

2010

continued from 169

FOR THE FILLING

½ cup butter, softened

2 teaspoons finely chopped fresh rosemary

3 cloves garlic, minced

½ cup grated Parmesan cheese

MAKE THE FILLING:

In a medium bowl, stir together the softened butter, rosemary, and garlic; spread over the surface of the dough. Sprinkle evenly with the Parmesan.

Starting at one of the long sides, roll up the dough tightly into a log, pinching the edge to seal. Place the log seam-side down on the work surface. With a sharp knife, cut the log in half lengthwise, cutting through the layers of dough. Lay the two dough halves side by side, cut-sides up. Twist the two halves together to create a "braid." Keeping the cut-sides up, form the braid into a circle; pinch the ends together.

Transfer the loaf to the prepared skillet. Cover and let rise in a warm place until doubled in size, 30 to 45 minutes.

Heat the oven to 375°F. Bake the loaf until golden brown, 30 to 40 minutes. Cover with foil for the last 10 minutes of baking to prevent overbrowning. Serve warm or at room temperature.

SUNDROP FLOWER SIPPER

Rapunzel's hair may be magical, but that magic came from a single drop of sunlight that fell to the ground and grew into a beautiful golden flower. This delightful yellow drink—topped with an edible yellow flower—celebrates that magical drop of sunlight!

DRINK ✦ GF, V, V+ ✦ YIELD: 2 drinks

FOR THE GINGER-BASIL SYRUP

½ cup water

¼ cup raw (demerara) or granulated sugar

2 thin slices of fresh gingerroot

4 large basil leaves

FOR THE DRINK

Two 6-ounce cans 100% pineapple juice, chilled

Ice cubes

2 lime wedges

One 12-ounce can or bottle ginger beer, chilled (see note)

FOR SERVING

2 yellow edible nasturtium blossoms

> **NOTE:**
> Ginger beer is non-alcoholic.

MAKE THE GINGER-BASIL SYRUP:

In a small saucepan, combine the water and sugar over medium heat. Heat, stirring constantly, until the sugar is dissolved. Remove from the heat and stir in the gingerroot and basil. Let steep for 10 minutes. Strain the syrup into a glass jar and cool completely.

MAKE THE DRINK:

In a small pitcher, combine the ginger-basil syrup and pineapple juice. Place 2 large ice cubes in each of two cocktail glasses. Squeeze a lime wedge over each glass and drop into the glasses. Pour the pineapple mixture over the ice. Pour the ginger beer into the glasses and garnish with nasturtium blossoms.

2010

SUGAR RUSH LOLLIPOPS

If there's one thing Vanellope von Schweetz knows, it's candy. This feisty racer makes her home in the video game *Sugar Rush,* which features a land made entirely of sugary treats such as gumdrops and peppermints. Why, even her wand is just a giant lollipop!

DESSERT ✦ GF, V, V+ ✦ YIELD: 12 lollipops

12 lollipop sticks

Vegetable oil, for greasing the foil

2 cups granulated sugar

1 cup light-colored corn syrup

¼ cup water

1 teaspoon desired extract flavoring: root beer, cherry, or lemon

½ teaspoon liquid food coloring in color of choice (optional)

Candy sprinkles

Arrange the lollipop sticks 3 inches apart on two greased, foil-lined baking sheets.

In a large, heavy saucepan, combine the sugar, corn syrup, and water. Bring to a boil over medium-high heat, stirring frequently. Cover, lower the heat to medium, and cook for 3 minutes. Uncover and clip a candy thermometer to the pan. Increase the heat to medium-high and cook, stirring constantly, until the thermometer reaches 310°F, hard crack stage.

Remove from the heat. Stir in the flavoring and food coloring, if desired. Carefully pour onto prepared baking sheets over the lollipop sticks, making 2-inch candy circles.

Immediately sprinkle with candy sprinkles, pressing into the soft candy before they harden (which usually takes 30 to 45 minutes).

2012

SCANDINAVIAN PANCAKES WITH LINGONBERRY JAM

Coronation Day in Arendelle means thousands of people streaming through the city gates. These traditional Scandinavian pancakes are sure to be on the top of every visitor's must-eat list. After all, it's not every day you get a Norwegian crepe fresh off the griddle!

ENTRÉE (BREAKFAST) ✦ V
YIELD: 4 (3-pancake) servings

FOR THE WHIPPED CREAM

1 cup heavy whipping cream, chilled

1 tablespoon granulated sugar

FOR THE PANCAKES

1 cup whole milk

4 large eggs

1 tablespoon granulated sugar

¼ teaspoon salt

½ teaspoon vanilla extract

⅔ cup all-purpose flour

2 tablespoons butter, melted

FOR SERVING

Lingonberry preserves

MAKE THE WHIPPED CREAM:

In a medium bowl, beat the cream and sugar with an electric mixer just until stiff peaks form, 5 to 6 minutes. Cover and chill until serving.

MAKE THE PANCAKES:

In a large bowl, whisk together the milk, eggs, sugar, salt, and vanilla. Whisk in the flour until the batter is smooth and no lumps remain. (Batter will be thin.)

Heat a medium nonstick skillet over medium-low heat. Brush the skillet with a small amount of the butter. Pour a scant ¼ cup of batter into heated skillet, quickly tilting the skillet to coat the entire bottom of the skillet with a thin layer of batter.

Cook until the bottom of the pancake is lightly browned, 30 to 60 seconds. Use a long metal spatula to flip the pancake. Cook for another 30 seconds. Remove the pancake to a plate. Repeat with the remaining butter and batter, stacking the pancakes as you go.

Serve the pancakes rolled or folded, topped with lingonberry preserves, and whipped cream.

2013

ICICLE COOKIES

When Elsa accidentally freezes Arendelle, the fjord is instantly covered in a sheet of ice and the forest hangs with beautiful, sparkling icicles. Celebrate the beauty of Elsa's ice powers with these snow-and-ice-crusted cookies, sure to put you in the mood for winter!

DESSERT ✦ V ✦ YIELD: About 2 dozen cookies

FOR THE COOKIES

2½ cups all-purpose flour

½ teaspoon baking soda

1 large egg

½ cup sour cream

¼ cup milk

1 cup granulated sugar

1 tablespoon butter, melted

⅛ teaspoon anise extract or vanilla extract

Coarse sanding sugars in white, blue, lavender

FOR THE POWDERED SUGAR ICING

2 cups sifted powdered sugar

2 tablespoons milk, plus more as needed

1 tablespoon light corn syrup

½ teaspoon vanilla extract

MAKE THE COOKIES:

In a small bowl, stir together the flour and baking soda; set aside.

In a large bowl, beat together the egg, sour cream, milk, and sugar. Beat in the butter and extract. Gradually stir in the flour mixture. Wrap the dough in plastic wrap. Chill in the refrigerator for 3 hours or overnight, until firm enough to handle and not too sticky.

Heat the oven to 400°F. Line a large rimmed baking pan with parchment paper.

Portion out several 1-tablespoon balls of dough. On a very lightly floured surface, roll the balls of dough into 3-inch logs. Twist two logs together. Gently roll one end of the twist to taper into a point. Place on the prepared pan. Repeat with remaining dough, placing 2 inches apart.

Bake until set, 3 to 4 minutes. Turn on the broiler. Broil until just beginning to turn golden brown, about 1 minute. Remove from the oven and transfer to a wire rack to cool. Return the oven to 400°F. Repeat with remaining cookies.

MAKE THE POWDERED SUGAR ICING:

In a medium bowl, stir together the powdered sugar, milk, light corn syrup, and vanilla extract. Stir in additional milk, 1 teaspoon at a time, until icing is of spreading consistency.

When the cookies are cool, brush the tops with powdered sugar icing and sprinkle with sanding sugars. Let icing dry completely before storing in an airtight container at room temperature for up to 1 week.

2013

FACE-NUMBING CHICKEN WINGS

Being a kid is tough, but Aunt Cass knows that a surefire way to brighten Hiro's day is with a plate of his favorite: chicken wings with a sauce hot enough to numb his face! Inspired by Aunt Cass's special recipe, these wings are sure to revitalize anyone's bad day!

APPETIZER/SNACK ✦ GF ✦ YIELD: 4 to 6 servings

FOR THE WINGS

2 pounds whole chicken wings

¼ cup cornstarch

2 teaspoons crushed red pepper flakes

½ teaspoon ground white pepper

½ teaspoon freshly ground Sichuan peppercorns

¾ teaspoon ground cumin

½ teaspoon paprika

½ teaspoon salt

¼ teaspoon granulated sugar

6 cups vegetable oil, for frying

FOR THE SAUCE

½ cup butter

⅓ cup garlic-chile sauce

¼ cup water

2 tablespoons brown sugar

1 tablespoon hoisin sauce

1 teaspoon toasted sesame oil

Few dashes sriracha sauce (optional)

½ teaspoon garlic powder

¼ teaspoon salt

FOR SERVING

Sesame seeds and chopped green onion, for garnish

MAKE THE CHICKEN:

Pat the chicken dry with paper towels; set aside.

In a large bowl, combine the cornstarch, crushed red pepper flakes, white pepper, Sichuan peppercorns, cumin, paprika, salt, and sugar. Add the chicken wings and toss to coat. Cover and marinate in the refrigerator for at least 2, or up to 24, hours.

Remove the chicken from the refrigerator and let it stand at room temperature for 30 minutes. Place a wire rack on a large rimmed baking pan. Cover the rack with paper towels.

In a large pot or deep fryer, heat the oil to 325°F. Add 3 pieces of the chicken to the oil. Fry until crispy and golden brown, 6 to 8 minutes. Remove with a slotted spoon and place on the paper-towel-covered rack. Return the oil to 325°F. Repeat frying remaining chicken.

MAKE THE SAUCE:

In a large skillet, melt the butter over medium heat. Add the chile sauce, water, brown sugar, hoisin sauce, sesame oil, sriracha, if using, garlic powder, and salt. Bring the mixture to a simmer over medium heat, stirring occasionally.

Add the fried chicken wings to the skillet. Turn the wings over to coat with the sauce. Heat until the wings are heated through, 3 to 5 minutes.

Transfer the wings to a serving platter. Sprinkle with the sesame seeds and green onions.

2014

HONEY-LEMON BEES KNEES

Honey Lemon is a brave and loyal member of Big Hero 6. A self-proclaimed chemistry whiz, she can whip up chem-balls for any occasion. Luckily, when she's not fighting bad guys, Honey Lemon is as sweet as her name. She's always looking on the bright side and ready for anything. You will be, too, after a taste of this honey-based beverage!

DRINK ✦ GF, V, V+ ✦ YIELD: 1 drink (enough syrup for 4 drinks)

FOR THE HONEY SYRUP

¼ cup honey

¼ cup boiling water

1 small sprig rosemary

FOR THE DRINK

Ice

2 ounces 100% pineapple juice

Freshly squeezed lemon juice

4 ounces sparkling water, chilled

Rosemary sprig

MAKE HONEY SYRUP:

In a small glass measuring cup, combine the honey and boiling water. Add the rosemary sprig. Let stand for 15 minutes. Remove the rosemary sprig and discard.

MAKE THE DRINK:

Fill a cocktail shaker with ice. Add 1 ounce of the honey syrup, the pineapple juice, and a splash of lemon juice. Shake well; strain into a coupe glass. Pour in the sparkling water. Garnish with a rosemary sprig.

2014

OVEN-BAKED CARROT CAKE DOUGHNUTS

As the only rabbit officer on the Zootopia police force, Judy Hopps has her work cut out for her when it comes to making friends. Luckily, she's found a way to at least one fellow officer's heart: doughnuts. These carrot cake doughnuts, inspired by Officer Clawhauser, are sure to make you plenty of true friends, too!

DESSERT ✦ V ✦ YIELD: 6 doughnuts

FOR THE DOUGHNUTS

Nonstick cooking spray

1 cup all-purpose flour

1 teaspoon pumpkin pie spice

½ teaspoon baking soda

¼ teaspoon baking powder

¼ teaspoon salt

1 large egg

⅓ cup granulated sugar

2 tablespoons brown sugar

¼ cup canola oil

2 tablespoons whole milk

Splash vanilla extract

¾ cup finely shredded carrots

¼ cup finely chopped walnuts

FOR THE GLAZE

4 ounces cream cheese, softened

3 tablespoons sifted powdered sugar

Splash vanilla extract

1 to 2 teaspoons milk

FOR SERVING

Finely chopped walnuts, sprinkles, and/or shredded carrot

MAKE THE DOUGHNUTS:

Heat the oven to 350°F. Spray a 6-cavity nonstick donut pan with nonstick cooking spray; set aside.

In a medium bowl, stir together the flour, pumpkin pie spice, baking soda, baking powder, and salt. In another medium bowl, whisk together the egg, granulated sugar, brown sugar, oil, milk, and vanilla. Add the egg mixture to the flour mixture. Stir with a wooden spoon until combined. Stir in the carrots and walnuts.

Spoon the batter into the prepared pan. Bake until a toothpick inserted in the center comes out clean, 12 to 15 minutes.

Invert the pan to release the doughnuts. Transfer to a wire rack to cool.

MAKE THE GLAZE:

In a medium bowl, beat the cream cheese, powdered sugar, and vanilla with an electric mixer until smooth. Beat in a teaspoon or two of milk if necessary to make a thick glaze. Spoon over the warm or cooled doughnuts.

Sprinkle the wet glaze with walnuts, sprinkles, and/or shredded carrot.

2016

NO-CHICKEN BOAT SNACK

When Maui finds Heihei hiding on Moana's ship, he's thrilled: Heihei looks to him like a ready-made meal, or "Boat Snack," in Maui's words. But Moana's not about to let anything bad happen to her friend. Crunchy and delicious, this No-Chicken Boat Snack is filling enough to keep even a demigod satisfied...for a while!

APPETIZER/SNACK ✦ V , V+ ✦ YIELD: 6 to 8 servings

FOR THE VEGETARIAN NO-CHICKEN BOUILLON POWDER

½ cup nutritional yeast

2 tablespoons salt

1 tablespoon garlic powder

1 tablespoon onion powder

1 tablespoon dried oregano

1 tablespoon dried basil

1 tablespoon dried thyme

2 teaspoons dried sage

2 teaspoons ground black pepper

½ teaspoon ground turmeric

FOR THE CRACKERS

One 9-ounce package oyster crackers

One 6.6-ounce package Parmesan-flavored, fish-shaped crackers

¼ cup butter

¼ cup canola oil

2 tablespoons dried parsley flakes

2 teaspoons poultry seasoning

MAKE THE VEGETARIAN NO-CHICKEN BOUILLON POWDER:

In a food processor bowl, combine the nutritional yeast, salt, garlic powder, onion powder, dried oregano, dried basil, dried thyme, dried sage, ground black pepper, and ground turmeric. Blend until a fine powder. Store in an airtight container.

MAKE THE CRACKERS:

Heat the oven to 300°F. In a large roasting pan, combine the oyster crackers and Parmesan fish-shaped crackers.

In a small saucepan, combine the butter, oil, 2 tablespoons vegetarian no-chicken bouillon powder, parsley flakes, and poultry seasoning. Cook over medium heat, stirring frequently, until warm and seasonings are aromatic, 3 to 4 minutes. Pour over the crackers. Toss to coat.

Bake for 10 minutes. Stir the crackers and bake for another 10 to 15 minutes or until golden brown. Cool completely.

2016

UNIFICATION SOUP

Chief Benja dreams of reuniting all his people—of finding a way to bring them together once more in the realm of Kumandra. But until he can find a way to do so, he'll have to be satisfied with uniting the flavors of Kumandra in a tasty soup that mixes the flavors of many different cultures together. This soup is inspired by something Chief Benja would whip up.

ENTRÉE ✦ GF* ✦ YIELD: 6 servings

2 tablespoons vegetable oil

8 ounces oyster mushrooms, cut up, or brown mushrooms, sliced

2 cloves garlic, minced

2 teaspoons minced fresh gingerroot

2 teaspoons minced lemongrass

4 cups chicken or vegetable broth

1 tablespoon chile paste

3 tablespoons rice vinegar

2 tablespoons soy sauce

1 teaspoon palm sugar or granulated sugar

12 ounces fresh or frozen medium shrimp, peeled and deveined

3 baby bok choy, halved, or 2 cups baby spinach

1 tablespoon cornstarch

1 tablespoon cold water

One 8-ounce can bamboo shoots, drained

2 green onions, sliced

Green onions, thinly sliced on the bias, for garnish

In a large pot, heat the oil over medium-high heat. Add the mushrooms and cook, stirring occasionally, for 3 to 4 minutes. Add the garlic, gingerroot, and lemongrass. Cook, stirring constantly, until fragrant, about 1 minute. Add the chicken broth, chile paste, vinegar, soy sauce, and sugar. Simmer, uncovered, for 5 minutes. Add the shrimp and bok choy. Simmer until the shrimp is opaque, 3 to 4 minutes.

In a small dish, stir together the cornstarch and cold water. Add to the saucepan; cook and stir for 1 to 2 minutes or until slightly thickened and clear.

Remove from the heat. Stir in the bamboo shoots and the 2 sliced green onions. Ladle into bowls and top with additional sliced scallions.

NOTE:
To make this dish gluten free, use a gluten-free soy sauce.

2021

SPRING ROLLS FOR TUK TUK

As the owner, manager, chef, and captain of the Shrimporium, Boun has learned how to make a lot of meals. Here, we have the classic spring roll, named after Raya's friend Tuk Tuk, who literally rolls from place to place.

APPETIZER/SNACK ✦ GF ✦ YIELD: 10 spring rolls

FOR THE ROLLS

1 ounce dried rice vermicelli noodles

1 cup shredded romaine or iceberg lettuce

½ cup shredded carrots

¼ cup thinly sliced basil leaves

¼ cup chopped fresh mint

2 tablespoons chopped cilantro

2 green onions, chopped

1 teaspoon lime zest

Ten 8-inch rice papers

Cilantro leaves

10 medium cooked shrimp, tails removed, halved

FOR THE DIPPING SAUCE

¼ cup water

3 tablespoons lime juice

2 teaspoons rice vinegar

1 tablespoon granulated sugar

1 teaspoon chile-garlic sauce

MAKE THE ROLLS:

Cook the noodles in boiling water for 3 to 5 minutes or until tender but firm. Drain and rinse with cold water; set aside. In a medium bowl, combine the lettuce, carrots, basil, mint, cilantro, green onions, and lime zest.

To assemble, pour about ½ cup warm water into a pie plate. Quickly dip a rice paper into the water and place on a dinner plate or clean work surface. Let stand a few seconds to soften. Place a few cilantro leaves in the center of the rice paper. Arrange 2 shrimp halves on top of the cilantro leaves. Place about ⅓ cup of the lettuce mixture just below the center of the rice paper. Arrange some of the vermicelli noodles across the lettuce mixture. Tightly roll up the rice paper from the bottom, tucking in the sides as you roll.

Repeat with the remaining rice papers, cilantro, shrimp, lettuce, and vermicelli. Serve with the dipping sauce.

MAKE THE DIPPING SAUCE:

In a small bowl, combine the water, lime juice, rice vinegar, sugar, and chile sauce.

2021

MAGICAL AREPAS

As a parent, there's no doubt that Julieta's food is filled with love. But her food is filled with something else, too: magic. More specifically, healing magic. One bite of her magical arepas is sure to cure any ailment, big or small! Inspired by Julieta's cooking, these arepas won't heal you, but they'll certainly warm your heart!

ENTRÉE ✦ GF ✦ YIELD: 4 to 6 servings

FOR THE SALSA

1 cup frozen corn kernels, thawed

2 Roma tomatoes, chopped

¼ cup sliced black olives

¼ cup chopped red onion

1 jalapeño, seeded and finely chopped

1 tablespoon fresh lime juice

1 tablespoon corn oil

½ teaspoon salt

FOR THE CORN CAKES

1½ cups masarepa (see note)

1½ cups warm water

½ teaspoon salt

1 tablespoon corn oil or vegetable oil, plus more for greasing

4 ounces sliced Oaxaca or mozzarella cheese

NOTES:

Masarepa is a precooked corn flour. Look for it online or at Latin American food markets. Regular corn flour cannot be substituted.

In addition to the cheese, try adding a couple of jalapeño slices or cilantro leaves when stuffing cakes.

MAKE THE SALSA:

In a small bowl, combine the corn, tomatoes, olives, onion, jalapeño, lime juice, oil, and salt. Cover and chill until serving time.

MAKE THE CORN CAKES:

In a large bowl, stir together the masarepa, water, salt, and corn oil. Knead the dough in the bowl until well combined. Let rest for 5 minutes.

Form the dough into 2-inch balls. Flatten the balls between pieces of parchment paper to ½-inch thickness.

Heat a griddle or nonstick skillet over medium-high heat. Brush the griddle with a little oil. Add a few corn cakes. Cook until lightly browned, about 3 minutes. Flip the cakes and cook until browned on both sides, 2 to 3 minutes more. Remove from the skillet. Repeat with the remaining patties.

To stuff cakes, split them in half horizontally. Place a cheese slice between the halves (see note). Return the cakes to the skillet. Cook until the cheese is melted, about 1 minute per side.

Serve the corn cakes with salsa.

2021

PROPOSAL DINNER SOUP

Being proposed to is supposed to be a magical moment, and doing it in front of family even more so. Isabela and Mariano's proposal dinner may not go according to plan, but at least the soup is good! Inspired by the soup served at the proposal dinner, this delicious chicken and corn soup is sure to lighten any mood!

ENTRÉE ✦ GF ✦ YIELD: 6 servings

FOR THE GUACAMOLE SALSA

1 ripe avocado, cut into pieces

2 tablespoons fresh lime juice

3 tablespoons chopped cilantro

2 tablespoons chopped red or white onion

1 serrano or jalapeño, finely chopped

Pinch of salt

1 to 2 tablespoons water (optional)

FOR THE SOUP

1½ pounds skinless, boneless chicken breast halves

3 cloves garlic, minced

5 green onions, washed and trimmed

2 tablespoons dried guascas (see note)

1 teaspoon ground black pepper, plus more to taste

1 teaspoon salt, plus more to taste

1 large russet potato, peeled and cut into 1½-inch pieces

4 cups chicken broth

¾ pound tiny golden potatoes

¾ pound tiny red or purple potatoes

3 ears fresh corn on cob

2 tablespoons capers

Sour cream or crème fraîche

MAKE THE GUACAMOLE SALSA:

In a blender or food processor, combine the avocado and lime juice. Add the cilantro, onion, pepper, and pinch of salt. Blend or process until nearly smooth. Add 1 or 2 tablespoons water, if necessary, to blend until smooth. Transfer to a serving bowl; cover and chill up to 2 hours.

MAKE THE SOUP:

In a large soup pot, combine the chicken, garlic, green onions, guascas, 1 teaspoon pepper, 1 teaspoon salt, and russet potato. Add 8 cups water and broth. Bring to a simmer over medium-high heat. Reduce heat; cover and simmer for 45 minutes.

Remove the green onions from the pot; discard. Transfer the chicken to a large bowl. Let cool for 5 to 10 minutes. Mash the potato pieces in the pot with a potato masher or a wooden spoon. Cut corn cobs in half crosswise. Shred the chicken and return to the pot along with the golden potatoes, red potatoes, and corn. Simmer, covered, for 20 minutes.

Stir in the capers. Season to taste with salt and pepper.

Divide the soup among 6 bowls, placing 1 corn cob half in each bowl. Serve with sour cream and guacamole salsa.

> ### NOTE:
> Guascas is a savory, mildly minty herb grown throughout South America. It is available online and at some Latin American food markets. If you don't have guascas, substitute 2 teaspoons dried oregano, 2 teaspoons dried parsley flakes, ½ teaspoon dried mint, and 2 bay leaves. Remove the bay leaves before serving.

2021

SPLAT PANCAKES

While exploring a strange underground world, Ethan meets Splat. Splat is a blobby blue creature who can flatten out like a pancake. Luckily, Ethan knows that Splat is a friend, not food! If only the Reapers understood that Ethan's not food either! Inspired by Splat, these pancakes make a great addition to any breakfast!

ENTRÉE (BREAKFAST) ✦ V
YIELD: 4 (3-pancake) servings

1 cup ricotta cheese

¾ cup whole milk

2 large eggs

3 tablespoons granulated sugar

3 tablespoons lemon juice

1 cup all-purpose flour

3 tablespoons freeze-dried blueberry powder

1 tablespoon baking powder

¼ teaspoon salt

1 teaspoon lemon zest

½ cup fresh or frozen blueberries

2 tablespoons butter, melted

Butter and pure maple syrup, for serving

Heat the oven to 200°F.

In a medium bowl, whisk together the ricotta, milk, eggs, sugar, and lemon juice. In a small bowl, combine the flour, blueberry powder, baking powder, and salt. Add the flour mixture to the ricotta mixture. Stir just until combined. Stir in the lemon zest and blueberries.

Heat a griddle or large nonstick skillet over medium heat. Brush with some of the melted butter. Spoon a scant ¼ cup of batter per pancake into the skillet, spreading the batter into irregular shapes. Cook until the bottoms are lightly browned and tops are bubbly, 1 to 2 minutes. Flip the pancakes over and cook for 1 minute more.

Transfer to a serving platter and repeat with the remaining batter and melted butter. (Keep cooked pancakes warm in the oven.)

Serve warm with additional butter and maple syrup.

2022

197

WISHING STAR COOKIES

What child hasn't wished upon a star? Asha certainly has. But when her wish is answered by a cosmic force called Star, she discovers that wishing can lead to truly wondrous things. These wishing star cookies remind all of us to keep wishing!

DESSERT ✦ V ✦ YIELD: About 5 dozen (2-inch) cookies

FOR THE COOKIES

1 cup unsalted butter, softened

1 cup granulated sugar

⅓ cup sour cream

1 large egg

1 teaspoon vanilla extract

1 tablespoon dried culinary lavender blossoms, crushed

3 cups all-purpose flour

¾ teaspoon baking powder

¼ teaspoon baking soda

¼ teaspoon salt

FOR THE ROYAL ICING

2 cups sifted powdered sugar

4 teaspoons meringue powder

½ teaspoon cream of tartar

¼ cup cold water, plus more as needed

Silver luster dust

MAKE THE COOKIES:

In a large bowl, beat the butter with an electric mixer for 30 seconds. Add the sugar, sour cream, egg, vanilla, and dried lavender. Beat until well combined, scraping the sides of the bowl with a rubber spatula as needed. Add the flour, baking powder, baking soda, and salt. Beat until combined. Divide the dough in half. Wrap and chill in the refrigerator until firm enough to roll out, at least 2 hours or overnight.

Heat the oven to 375°F. Line 2 large rimmed baking pans with parchment paper.

On a lightly floured surface, roll out half of the dough to ¼-inch thickness. Using a 2-inch, star-shaped cookie cutter, cut out the dough and place 1 inch apart on the prepared baking pans. Reroll scraps and repeat with all the dough.

Bake until the edges are firm and bottoms are very lightly browned, 7 to 8 minutes. Transfer the cookies to a wire rack to cool. Repeat with remaining dough.

MAKE THE ROYAL ICING:

In a medium bowl, combine the powdered sugar, meringue powder, and cream of tartar. Add the water. Beat with an electric mixer on low speed until combined. Beat on high speed until thick and fluffy, 4 to 5 minutes. On low speed, mix in enough additional water to thin the frosting to an icing consistency that flows, 2 to 3 tablespoons.

To decorate, spread the royal icing over the top of the cookies. Let dry until the icing is hard, at least 2 hours. When dry, use a clean, dry artist's brush to dry-paint luster dust onto the iced cookies.

2023

SUGGESTED MENUS

COZY WINTER NIGHT

Alponian Chowder
with Extra
Solaris Seed (page 141)

Buttermilk-Honey Skillet
Cornbread (page 25)

Mixed green salad

Kitty-Cat
Snaps (page 92)

Sleepy Chamomile Tea
Latte (page 70)

HAPPY HOLIDAYS

Roquefort Blue Cheese
Wheels (page 83)

Chocolate Pot Roast with
Green Gravy (page 44)

"No Worries" Mashed
Potatoes (page 114)

Steamed green beans

Icicle Cookies (page 178)

Black Forest Hot
Cocoa (page 32)

PERFECT PICNIC

Golden Touch
Roasted Chicken
(page 27, see note)

Deli potato salad

Spring Salad with Green
Goddess Dressing
(page 26, see note)

The Big Olive
Bread (page 125)

Queen of Hearts Jam
Tarts (page 57)

Lemonade and iced tea

NOTES: Omit the rice
from the Golden Touch
Roasted Chicken. Bake
the chicken, then cool
completely. Wrap tightly
in foil, then chill at least
4 hours or overnight.
Transport chicken in
a cooler packed with
ice. Enjoy cold.

**FOR THE SPRING
SALAD WITH GREEN
GODDESS DRESSING:**
Make the dressing. Toss all
of the vegetables for the
salad together in a large
container with a cover.
Keep dressing and salad
separate until serving
time. Transport in a cooler
packed with ice.

SPECIAL BIRTHDAY

Hot Hors d'Oeuvres
Gougères (page 106)

Straw and Hay
Pasta (page 22)

Mixed green salad

Very Tall Buttercream
Birthday Cake (page 66)

Mermaid's Kiss (page 101)

AFTERNOON TEA

Deli chicken salad tea
sandwiches (see note)

Wild Chase Tea
Biscuits (page 47)

Fresh grapes

Tarte aux
Fraises (page 109)

Mrs. Potts
Special-Tea (page 109)

NOTE: Spread purchased
chicken salad on a slice
of soft white bread. Top
with a second slice of
bread. Trim crusts, then
cut into 4 triangles to
make 4 tea sandwiches.
Repeat as necessary.

GAME TIME

Disappearing
Wizard Mix (page 77)

Face-Numbing Chicken
Wings (page 181)

NYC Pup Cart
Chile Dogs (page 97)

Veggies and dip

Friendship-Building
Peanut Bars (page 42)

FUNTIME BRUNCH

Waffle World Chicken and
Waffles (page 157)

Special-Treat
Greens (page 43)

Fresh fruit salad

Bare Necessities Banana
Muffins (page 78)

Sundrop Flower
Sipper (page 173)

DISHES BY CATEGORY

DIETARY CONSIDERATIONS

KEY

V: VEGETARIAN   **V+:** VEGAN   **V+*:** EASILY MADE VEGAN   **GF:** GLUTEN-FREE   **GF*:** EASILY MADE GLUTEN-FREE

CHAPTER 1:
1930s-1949

Louisiana Fries: **GF, V**

Straw and Hay Pasta: **V**

Buttermilk-Honey
Skillet Cornbread: **V**

Spring Salad with
Green Goddess
Dressing: **GF, V, V+***

Golden Touch
Roasted Chicken: **GF**

Safe-to-Eat
Apple Strudel: **V**

Black Forest
Hot Cocoa: **GF, V**

Tuscan Roast Chicken: **GF**

Waltz of the
Flowers Fairy Cake: **V**

The Sorcerer's Apprentice
Wizard-Hat Cupcakes: **V**

Friendship-Building
Peanut Bars: **V**

Special-Treat
Greens: **GF*, V**

Chocolate Pot Roast with
Green Gravy: **GF**

Wild Chase Tea Biscuits: **V**

Sleepy Hollow-een
Pumpkin Cupcakes: **V**

CHAPTER 2:
1950-1969

Mouse-Approved
Cheesy Corn Puffs: **V**

Bibbidi-Bobbidi
Blueberry Tarts: **V**

Queen of
Hearts Jam Tarts: **V**

Cheshire Cat
Grin: **GF, V, V+**

Tick-Tock Croc
Drink: **GF, V, V+**

Crispy Oven-
Fried Codfish: **GF***

Good-Doggie Doughnuts: **V**

Very Tall Buttercream
Birthday Cake: **V**

Sleepy Chamomile Tea
Latte: **GF, V, V+***

Towering Roast
Beef Sandwiches

Disappearing Wizard Mix: **V**

Bare Necessities
Banana Muffins: **V**

CHAPTER 3:
1970-1989

Roquefort Blue
Cheese Wheels: **V**

Coin Cookies: **V**

Smackerel
of Honeycakes: **V**

Blustery Day
Carrot Soup: **GF, V**

Kitty-Cat Snaps: **V**

Porcupine-Shaped
Meatballs: **GF***

NYC Pup Cart Chili Dogs

Under the Sea Curried
Crab-Free Dumplings: **V, V+**

Mermaid's Kiss: **GF, V, V+**

CHAPTER 4:
1990-1999

Soup du Jour: **V**

Hot Hors
d'Oeuvres Gougères: **V**

Tarte aux Fraises with Mrs.
Potts Special-Tea: **V**

Arabian Moon Cookies: **V**

"No Worries" Mashed
Potatoes: **GF, V**

Pecans with a Very
Pleasant Crunch: **GF, V**

Three Sisters
Succotash: **GF, V**

Feast of Fools
Topsy-Turvy Cake: **V**

The Big Olive Bread: **V, V+**

Happy-to-See-You Porridge

Ginger-Pork Dumplings

CHAPTER 5:
2000-2009

Roasted Purple Peruvian
Potatoes: **GF, V, V+**

Mudka's Meat
Hut Meat Mug: **GF**

Road-to-Atlantis
Turkey Jerky: **GF***

Lū'au Blue Hawaiian
Drink:: **GF, V, V+**

Polynesian Sweet
Potatoes: **GF, V**

Alponian Chowder with
Extra Solaris Seed

Bonzabeast Stew

Nut-Crusted Salmon with
Cranberry Relish: **GF***

Little Patch of Heaven
Custard Pie: **V**

Commander Little
Hero Sandwich: **V**

Meatball Cannon
Meatballs in Gravy

Waffle World
Chicken and Waffles

Best Gumbo
You've Ever Tasted

Louis Muffulettas

Big Daddy Beignets: **V**

CHAPTER 6:
2010-Present

Parmesan-Garlic Braided
Skillet Bread: **V**

Sundrop Flower
Sipper: **GF, V, V+**

Sugar Rush
Lollipops: **GF, V, V+**

Scandinavian Pancakes with
Lingonberry Jam: **V**

Icicle Cookies: **V**

Face-Numbing
Chicken Wings: **GF**

Honey-Lemon Bees
Knees: **GF, V, V+**

Oven-Baked Carrot
Cake Doughnuts: **V**

No-Chicken
Boat Snack: **V, V+**

Unification Soup: **GF***

Spring Rolls for Tuk Tuk: **GF**

Magical Arepas: **GF**

Proposal Dinner Soup: **GF**

Splat Pancakes: **V**

Wishing Star Cookies: **V**

GLOSSARY

BEAT: To blend ingredients and/or incorporate air into a mixture by vigorously whisking, stirring, or using a handheld or stand mixer.

BLANCH AND SHOCK: Blanching is the process of bringing water to a boil, adding food, most commonly vegetables or fruits, to the water, and cooking for a quick time, normally 1 to 3 minutes. To stop the cooking process from going too far, the food is removed from the boiling water and plunged into an ice bath (½ water and ½ ice) to cool before it is drained and used in the recipe.

BLOOMING GELATIN: Blooming gelatin helps ensure the gelatin will dissolve easily and create a smooth finished product. Using the amount of water and gelatin asked for in the recipe, place the water in a shallow bowl and sprinkle the gelatin evenly over the surface. Allow the gelatin to bloom for 3 to 5 minutes. Visually, you will see the changes as the gelatin begins to absorb the water and swell.

CHIFFONADE: This French term means "little ribbons." It is the method of taking leaves, such as basil, and stacking them together, rolling them up, and then thinly slicing them to create thin ribbons of garnish.

CUTTING IN BUTTER: To work cold butter into dry ingredients until it is broken down into small pea-size pieces and dispersed evenly throughout the mixture.

It is important that the butter is very cold so it does not begin to soften. These little pieces of butter surrounded by the dry ingredient are what create the flakiness in pastry.

DEGLAZE: Deglazing is adding liquid, usually wine or stock, to a hot pan to release all of the caramelized food from the pan. These caramelized bits, called fond, are full of flavor and should not be left behind. Deglazing is often the first step in making a delicious sauce.

FOLDING IN: This refers to gently adding an ingredient with a spatula in wide gentle strokes. Do not whisk or stir vigorously. Folding allows any airiness already established to stay intact.

FRY STATION SAFETY: If you're making something that requires deep frying, here are some important tips to prevent you from setting your house (and yourself) on fire.

• If you don't have a dedicated deep fryer, use a Dutch oven or a high-walled sauté pan.

• Never have too much oil in the pan! You don't want hot oil spilling out as soon as you put the food in.

• Only use a suitable cooking oil, like canola, peanut, or vegetable oil.

• Always keep track of the oil temperature with a thermometer; 350°F to 375°F should do the trick.

• Never put too much food in the pan at the same time!

• Never put wet food in the pan. It will splatter and may cause burns.

• Always have a lid nearby to cover the pan in case it starts to spill over or catch fire. A properly rated fire extinguisher is also great to have on hand in case of emergencies.

• Never leave the pan unattended, and never let children near the pan.

• Never, ever put your face, hand, or any other body part in the hot oil.

GREASING A PAN: Coating a pan with nonstick cooking spray, oil, softened butter, or shortening in order to keep (usually) baked goods such as cakes from sticking.

MACERATE: Fruit mixed with sugar and/or some citrus juice is set aside to soften and release its natural juices. This is known as macerating.

PIPING FROSTING: The process of decorating cakes and cookies by squeezing frosting placed in a decorating bag over them. Piping can be done with or without a decorating tip—or even in a plastic bag with one corner snipped off to allow the frosting to be applied in a neat rope shape.

SEAR: To create a crust on a piece of meat, poultry, or fish by placing it in a very hot pan or on a very hot grill. The high heat quickly caramelizes the natural sugars in the food, creating a deeply browned and flavorful crust. Once the crust is formed, the heat is usually turned down so that the interior of the meat can cook properly before the outside is burned.

SHIMMERING OIL: Shimmering oil is hot but not to smoke point. You know it's "shimmering" when it spreads out quickly across the pan, has a rippled look across the surface, and glistens.

SIFT: The process of putting flour, powdered sugar, or cornstarch through a fine-mesh sieve in order to aerate and remove lumps. Multiple ingredients—such as flour, salt, and leavenings—are often sifted together in order to blend them.

SIMMER: To cook a liquid such as a sauce or soup at low-enough heat so that bubbles are just barely breaking over the surface.

WHIP: To use a whisk or electric mixer to aerate ingredients such as egg whites and heavy cream in order to lighten, stiffen, and form peaks.

WHISK: To use a whisk (see definition under Helpful Tools), to combine ingredients or incorporate air into them.

ABOUT THE AUTHORS

BROOKE VITALE is a children's book editor and the author of more than 100 books including *Goonies: The Illustrated Storybook*, *The Muppet's Christmas Carol: An illlustrated Classic*, *Slushy, Slurpy City Snow*, and *The Magic Is in You*. Brooke lives in Connecticut with her husband and two sons. Visit Brooke at brookevitale.com.

LISA KINGSLEY has more than 30 years' experience as a food writer, editor, and recipe developer. Her work has appeared in magazines such as *Fine Cooking* and *Better Homes & Gardens*. She collaborated with the Smithsonian Institution on *American Table: The Foods, People, and Innovations That Feed Us* (Harvest, 2023).

JENNIFER PETERSON has been food styling and developing recipes for more than 25 years. Her magazine work includes *Fine Cooking*, *Better Homes & Gardens*, and *Forks Over Knives*, among others. Her food styling has appeared in *Emily in Paris: The Official Cookbook*, *Disney Princess Tea Parties*, *Disney Villains: Devilishly Delicious Cookbook*, and *Star Wars Galactic Baking*. Her baking specialties include wedding cakes and gingerbread houses.

ACKNOWLEDGMENTS

BROOKE VITALE: To my two boys, Sammy and Alex, who keep me on my toes when it comes to creative meals!

LISA KINGSLEY: To Hannah and Emma, remembering all of the fun and cozy nights we spent watching Disney movies and eating yummy food.

JENNIFER PETERSON: To my 18-month-old granddaughter, Adeline, who is already a huge fan of Minnie Mouse ("Mimi").

METRIC CONVERSION CHART

KITCHEN MEASUREMENTS

CUPS	TABLESPOONS	TEASPOONS	FLUID OUNCES
1/16 cup	1 tablespoon	3 teaspoons	1/2 fluid ounce
1/8 cup	2 tablespoons	6 teaspoons	1 fluid ounce
1/4 cup	4 tablespoons	12 teaspoons	2 fluid ounces
1/3 cup	5 1/2 tablespoons	16 teaspoons	2 2/3 fluid ounces
1/2 cup	8 tablespoons	24 teaspoons	4 fluid ounces
2/3 cup	10 2/3 tablespoons	32 teaspoons	5 1/3 fluid ounces
3/4 cup	12 tablespoons	36 teaspoons	6 fluid ounces
1 cup	16 tablespoons	48 teaspoons	8 fluid ounces

GALLONS	QUARTS	PINTS	CUPS	FLUID OUNCES
1/16 gallon	1/4 quart	1/2 pint	1 cup	8 fluid ounces
1/8 gallon	1/2 quart	1 pint	2 cups	16 fluid ounces
1/4 gallon	1 quart	2 pints	4 cups	32 fluid ounces
1/2 gallon	2 quarts	4 pints	8 cups	64 fluid ounces
1 gallon	4 quarts	8 pints	16 cups	128 fluid ounces

WEIGHT

GRAMS	OUNCES
14 grams	½ ounce
28 grams	1 ounce
57 grams	2 ounces
85 grams	3 ounces
113 grams	4 ounces
142 grams	5 ounces
170 grams	6 ounces
283 grams	10 ounces
397 grams	14 ounces
454 grams	16 ounces
907 grams	32 ounces

OVEN TEMPERATURES

FAHRENHEIT	CELSIUS
200°F	93°C
225°F	107°C
250°F	121°C
275°F	135°C
300°F	149°C
325°F	163°C
350°F	177°C
375°F	191°C
400°F	204°C
425°F	218°C
450°F	232°C

LENGTH

IMPERIAL	METRIC
1 inch	2.5 centimeters
2 inches	5 centimeters
4 inches	10 centimeters
6 inches	15 centimeters
8 inches	20 centimeters
10 inches	25 centimeters
12 inches	30 centimeters

INDEX

INSIGHT
EDITIONS

PO Box 3088
San Rafael, CA 94912
www.insighteditions.com

Find us on Facebook: www.facebook.com/InsightEditions

Follow us on Twitter: @insighteditions

Follow us on Instagram: @insighteditions

ISBN: 979-8-88663-199-9
Exlusive ISBN: 979-8-88663-514-0

INSIGHT EDITIONS
Publisher: Raoul Goff
VP, Co-Publisher: Vanessa Lopez
VP, Creative: Chrissy Kwasnik
VP, Manufacturing: Alix Nicholaeff
VP, Group Managing Editor: Vicki Jaeger
Publishing Director: Jamie Thompson
Art Director: Stuart Smith
Editor: Anna Wostenberg
Editorial Assistant: Sami Alvarado
Managing Editor: Maria Spano
Senior Production Editor: Katie Rokakis
Production Associate: Deena Hashem
Senior Production Manager, Subsidiary Rights: Lina s Palma-Temena

WATERBURY PUBLICATIONS, INC.
Editorial Director: Lisa Kingsley
Creative Director: Ken Carlson
Associate Art Director: Doug Samuelson
Photographer: Ken Carlson
Food Stylist: Jennifer Peterson
Food Stylist Assistant: Holly Wiederin

ROOTS of PEACE   REPLANTED PAPER

Insight Editions, in association with Roots of Peace, will plant two trees for each tree
used in the manufacturing of this book. Roots of Peace is an internationally renowned
humanitarian organization dedicated to eradicating land mines worldwide and
converting war-torn lands into productive farms and wildlife habitats. Roots of Peace
will plant two million fruit and nut trees in Afghanistan and provide farmers there with
the skills and support necessary for sustainable land use.

Manufactured in China by Insight Editions

10 9 8 7 6 5 4 3 2 1